THE DRIVER'S MIRROR

Looking at Your Driving
And That of Others

The Psychology of Driving

by

Dr. Elwin G. Upton, M.D., F.R.C.P.(C).

The Driver's Mirror

Copyright © 2011 Dr. Elwin Upton, M.D., F.R.C.P.(C.)

ALL RIGHTS RESERVED.

No part of this publication may be reproduced, stored in a retrieval system, or transmitted, in any form or by any means, electronic, mechanical, photocopying, recording or otherwise without the prior permission of the publisher in writing.

The information, views, opinions and visuals expressed in this publication are solely those of the author(s) and do not reflect those of the publisher. The publisher disclaims any liabilities or responsibilities whatsoever for any damages, libel or liabilities arising directly or indirectly from the contents of this publication.

ISBN 978-1-742841-10-6 (pbk.)

First edition

Publisher: Bookpal
www.bookpal.com.au

Cover design by Dr. Elwin G. Upton, M.D., F.R.C.P.(C.)

The Driver's Mirror

DEDICATION

TO MY DECEASED GRANDMOTHERS, ONE OF WHOM WAS NEARLY KILLED IN MY YOUTH BY AN IRRESPONSIBLE TRUCK DRIVER, MY PARENTS, BOTH EXCELLENT DRIVERS, MY WONDERFUL WIFE, WHO UNFAILINGLY COMMENTS WHEN MY OWN DRIVING IS AN ISSUE AND TO ALL MATURE, THOUGHTFUL, RESPONSIBLE DRIVERS WHO DO NOT TAKE PRIVILEGES FOR GRANTED AND SHOW RESPECT AND CONSIDERATION FOR OTHER ROAD USERS.

The Driver's Mirror

ACKNOWLEDGEMENTS

Many thanks to my friends Grant and Glenys Watt for honest and invaluable comments and suggestions, to work colleagues, Edwina Milner, Suicide Intervention Worker, O.T., Sarah Chamberlain and husband, Terrence Boylen, photographer and multi-talented fellow, and her brother, First Class Constable David Chamberlain, for feedback and to my many clients and patients, whose often tragic stories related to driving calamities have painfully informed me of the sometimes horrible and far-reaching consequences of motor vehicle accidents.

The Driver's Mirror

CONTENTS

P. 3-5

P. 6-8   **Preface**

P. 9-14   **The Driver's Mirror Introduction**
          Psychology & Psychological Issues In Driving

P. 15   **Necessary Conditions For Safe Driving**

P. 16-35   **Issues Compromising A Safe Driving Experience**

P.16, 17	Poor Training & Preparation For Driving
P.18, 19	Acting-Out Behaviours
P.19-25	Impairments
P.25-31	Poor Judgment
P.31-33	Limited Insight Into Or Concern For The Psychology Of The Driving Situation
P.34-35	Limited Insight Into Or Concern About Responsibilities & Consequences

P.36-37   **Common Causes Of Avoidable Mishaps And Associated Psychology**

P.38-40   **The Psychology Of Speeding**

P.40-43   **Behaviours and Psychological Issues Associated With Being Caught**

P.43, 44   **The Psychology Of Risk-Taking Behaviour**

P.44-49   **Problem Drivers With Psychological Issues**

P.50-60   **Interactions With Other Drivers**
P.51-54	Illustrative Examples and Traffic Games
P.54-58	Defensive Driving
P.58-60	Antisocial Plotting/Colluding

The Driver's Mirror

P.61-66 Psychological And Physical Consequences Of Problem Driving

    Illustrative Scenarios

P.66-74 Other Aspects of Driving Influenced By Psychology

P.66-68	The Psychology of the Timing and Circumstances of License Acquisition
P.69-72	The Psychology of the Timing and Circumstances of Driving Cessation
P.73	Selection of a Vehicle & Susceptibility to Sales Strategies
P.74	The Decision to Drive Rather Than Use Public Transportation

P.75-97 Driving Situations and Problem Driving Behaviours

P.75	Entering a Public Road
P.75	Approaching a Traffic-Light-Regulated Intersection
P.76	Behaviour at a Traffic-Light-Regulated Intersection
P.76	Approaching an Unregulated Intersection
P.77	Behaviour at an Unregulated Intersection
P.77	Negotiating a Traffic Circle/Roundabout
P.78	Driving in a One-Lane-Bridge/One-Shared-Lane Situation
P.78	Driving in a One-Way Situation
P.79	Driving in a One-Forward-Lane Situation
P.79	Driving in a Multi-Forward-Lane Situation
P.80	Entering an Expressway, Freeway or Dual Carriage Way
P.80	Driving on an Expressway, Freeway or Dual Carriage Way
P.80	Approaching a Merging-Lane Situation
P.81	Exiting an Expressway, Freeway or Dual Carriage Way

The Driver's Mirror

P.81	Bus/Train/Airport Drop-Off/Pickup Situations
P.82	Designated Parking Parallel to a One- or Two-Forward-Lane Situation
P.83	Undesignated Parking Parallel to a One- or Two-Forward-Lane Situation
P.83	Parking in a Designated Parking Lot/Garage with Designated Bays
P.83	Parking in a Designated Parking Lot/Garage with Undesignated Bays
P.84	Parking in a Reverse-in-Angle-Parking Situation
P.84	Parking in an Undesignated Parking Situation
P.85	Parking on a Hill/Steep Slope
P.85	Other Parking Situations
P.85-88	Other Circumstances
P.89-92	Antisocial Driving Behaviours
P.93	Non-Courteous Driving Behaviours
P.93,94	Interactions with Police
P.94,95	Interactions with Emergency/Military Personnel/Vehicles and/or Road Workers
P.95	Emergency Situations – (Not Everyone in the World Has a Mobile Phone!)
P.96, 97	Natural-Emergency Situations

P.97-102 Problem Driving Behaviours Which Reveal Biases/Prejudices

P.98	Sexist Driving
P.99	Racist/Culturally-Biased Driving
P.99	Age Issues
P.100-102	Other Cues to Which the Driver May React With Bias, Prejudice, Acting-out or Problem Behaviours

P.103-109 Driving-Contemplation Checklist

P.110, 111 Conclusion

The Driver's Mirror

Preface

This manual is to be studied in conjunction with the Road Rules, Manual of Licensing Requirements and Educational Materials regarding driving, provided in your jurisdiction. These publications usually emphasise information about safe driving, how to obtain a drivers license, information about the rules of the road and safety issues, information about legal issues and traffic violations and information about emergencies. **This** publication emphasises the various issues which can compromise the driving experience, the **universal involvement of psychological issues in every aspect of the driving experience**, the physical and psychological consequences when things go wrong and dozens of examples of what **not** to do while driving.

It is meant

- to increase the awareness and education of a prospective driver
- to remind a driver intending to renew a driver's license and/or an already-licensed driver regarding his or her many responsibilities and of the various factors, especially **psychological issues**, which can play a very significant part in his or her driving behaviour and experience.

Although road conditions, quality of signage, topography, weather, mechanical road-worthiness of the vehicle and quality of the road surface, for example, all play a significant part in the driving experience,

THE MOST IMPORTANT DIMENSIONS DEFINING THE OUTCOME OF THE DRIVING EXPERIENCE ARE IN THE REALM OF THE MENTAL STATUS AND THE NATURE AND EXTENT OF THE PERSONAL PSYCHOLOGICAL ISSUES/PROBLEMS OF THE DRIVER AND OF ALL THE OTHER DRIVERS ENCOUNTERED AND THE WAY EACH MANAGES FEELINGS, IMPULSES AND PERSONAL ISSUES WHILE DRIVING

The Driver's Mirror

This manual has been written so as to be useful in whatever jurisdiction the driver drives. There are **two main driving systems** in the world, the **British and non-British systems**. In the British system, the steering column and driver's seat are on the right-hand side of the vehicle and the forward lanes are on the left of the roadway. In the non-British system, the steering column and driver's seat are on the left-hand side of the vehicle and the forward lanes are on the right of the roadway.

In each case, the driver is closer to the center line of the road. (Exceptions occur when the driver drives a vehicle with either a left-hand drive or right-hand drive in a place with the opposite system - **then beware at all times!**)

In a two-or-more-forward-lane situation, the **inside lane** is closest to the center of the road and the **outside lane** is closest to the shoulder of the road.

The purpose of this manual is to promote

- **awareness that driving on a public road is a privilege not a right**

- **good driving habits and behaviours**

- **respect for other drivers**

- **an attitude of sharing a positive driving experience with other drivers**

The Driver's Mirror

- increased awareness of when NOT to operate a vehicle

- increased self-awareness before and during the operation of a vehicle

- the elimination or significant reduction of acting-out and antisocial behaviours, and the associated often terrible consequences

- increased awareness of the projection of personal issues, biases and/or prejudices into the driving situation and consequences

- increased insight into personal psychology and the behaviour of other drivers

- increased awareness of psychological and/or physical consequences for self and others of problem driving

- greater understanding of the factors influencing timing of license acquisition and abandonment

- insight into the reasons for using the vehicle instead of public transportation

- realisation of the consequences for every action and decision

- review of a driving-readiness checklist

Happy Motoring !

The Driver's Mirror

The Driver's Mirror ...Looking At Your Driving and That Of Others

Modern day self-conducted motorised transportation is a multifaceted experience. One can go to places, see things and have experiences previously only imagined. Speed, unlimited visual opportunities and temperature-controlled comfort can make driving a stimulating, pleasant, and rewarding experience.

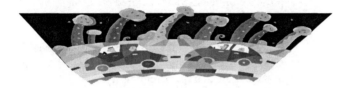

So why do we end up feeling hassled, frustrated, angry, afraid, anxious, disappointed, stressed-out or even endangered while driving?!

Blame the vagaries of human psychology!

Human beings invariably bring **psychological issues** into **every activity and situation**. Our thoughts, unresolved issues with self and others, unmet needs, beliefs, moods, urges, prejudices and perceptions of self and others, influence our behavior constantly.

We **project** our own issues, beliefs, moods, urges, prejudices and/or expectations into most situations and because of this, while driving for example, can even convince ourselves, **usually quite incorrectly**, that we even know what the other driver intends to do or not do, know what is in his or her mind and/or his or her intentions, and/or what he or she may think or feel about us!

Then, when we act on this basis, driving can become, often predictably and unfortunately , a contest, a competition, a frustration, an angry or dangerous encounter, a puzzling, frightening or anxiety-provoking experience and/or an occasion for psychological trauma, accidents, injury or death.

The Driver's Mirror

Personal psychological issues or problems arise in the context of the interaction amongst many factors.

This is not an exhaustive list! (The items with an asterisk will be further expanded below)

- the negative aspects of human nature and how these are managed*
- the presence of inherited or acquired medical/ psychiatric/ intellectual/behavioural characteristics, compromises or illnesses
- the beliefs, values, attitudes, problems, psychological/ physical health of the person's parenting figures, family, peers and culture and the parenting style
- the effects of childhood psychology on the interpretation of life events and aspects of parenting*
- the development of doubts and conflicts about self and others*
- the involvement of family/social/cultural/media/ national/international/historical/peer/religious/ philosophical issues
- the quality/sophistication of the educational system and the attitudes and psychological awareness of teachers
- the experience of adverse life events, such as neglect, abandonment, betrayal, prejudice, violence, threats, intimidation, physical/sexual/emotional abuse, losses, tragedies and disasters and how these are managed
- the sophistication of legal, political and health systems in the management of human issues
- the availability of resources/institutions/job opportunities and financial means to meet the many needs of the individual/family/group/society
- the manner in which the concepts of "stranger", "difference", "other", "foreigner" are introduced and managed

The Driver's Mirror

Some of the **negative aspects of human nature** which could play a part in the driving experience are **greed, jealousy, ability to rationalise every action/decision/belief/behaviour, envy, territoriality, aggressive and violent tendencies, selfishness, objectification of others, competitiveness, capacity to make excuses and for retribution, use of denial/fantasy/projection/passive-aggressive behaviour/acting-out and tendency to create hierarchies based on wealth, power and influence.**

If these issues are not managed in a mature, thoughtful, positive or humanitarian manner in the context of appropriate consequences, they could have a very negative effect on a person's attitude and behaviour while driving.

Adverse life events, including mistreatment by others, violence, victimisation, discrimination, bullying and/or a social environment promoting competitiveness, social stratification, gossip, tendencies to judge others, lack of consequences and/or adverse events in childhood, foster often deep-seated personal problems, resentments, strong negative feelings and/or problem attitudes and behaviours, all of which can enter the driving arena.

The Driver's Mirror

There are many theoretical explanations of the nature of childhood psychology, but distillation of these reveal certain essential aspects.

Childhood psychology can cause a child to believe that whatever is happening to his/her parenting figures, whatever behaviour, feelings and problems the parenting figures are showing/having, and whatever bad things are happening (conflict, yelling, abuse, punishment, unhappiness, substance abuse, poverty etc.) **must have something to do with him or her.**

That is to say, he or she **personalizes everything** and could conclude (if the parenting figures do not counteract such thoughts) that he or she **has done something** or **has not done something** which causes the behaviour, feelings or problems, or he or she **needs to do something** to fix the problem. These irrational interpretations and beliefs give rise to personal doubts and issues which can affect self-esteem, self-concept, feelings and behaviour, and the assessment of others, often for many years, even throughout the person's life. Personality disorder can result.

If a child is traumatised psychologically, the vulnerable aspects of child psychology can extend into adolescence and adulthood and can interfere with the transition to functional adult psychology and emotional maturity.

Personal doubts and doubtful perceptions of others, including dysfunctional parents, frightening strangers, and loud/rude/abusive/ neglectful/ hurtful people, can foster conflicts within the self and between the self and others.

The Driver's Mirror

The following is a list of areas in which a person can have issues with him/herself and/or with others

Acceptability
Acceptance and management of positive/negative feelings and/or aggressive impulses
Belongingness
Competence
Dependence/Independence
Desirability
Entitlement
Esteem
Identity
Individuation
Intelligence
Lovability/Likeability
Needs/Neediness/Being Needed
Power/Effectiveness
Procreation
Security
Sexuality
Trust
Worth

Being under the influence of doubts about oneself and others can have profound effects on the way a person approaches the driving experience, the interactions with other drivers, the inherent risks of driving and the responsibilities to adhere to the law and to appreciate and care about consequences.

The Driver's Mirror

The other complex and numerous issues which affect our psychology are equally important and far reaching. One can enquire into these issues by reading self-help books and psychology books.

We reflect our psychological issues, preferences, biases, beliefs, philosophies and prejudices not only in the way we **drive** a vehicle but also in the make, type and size of the vehicle we select, in its color, in the modifications we make to the vehicle (spoilers, air dams, wheel covers, roll/bull bars, custom-made holders and cabinets, low rider/high rider styling, racing modifications, loud mufflers) and in the manner in which it is adorned (with religious/cult/contemporary symbols, business and other advertising, racing stripes, fake or real bullet holes, nude male/female silhouettes, rude/crude/political/ humorous stickers, suggestive/personalized license plates, extra/colored lights, fuzzy animals and dolls, or other paraphernalia).

No matter what the vehicle looks like, however, the most important factors determining the quality and outcome of the driving experience are how our issues influence the way in which the vehicle is driven, how the vehicle is used in interactions with other drivers/other vehicles/pedestrians/ wildlife and whether the vehicle is operated within the requirements of the law and prevailing road and weather conditions.

The Driver's Mirror

NECESSARY CONDITIONS FOR SAFE DRIVING

1. Respect for road rules/conventions

2. Courtesy toward others

3. Respect for others, property, animals and wildlife

4. Awareness of the lethality of the vehicle

5. Awareness of the responsibility for proper on-going vehicle maintenance and seasonal readiness

6. Respect for and appropriate response to weather conditions

7. Constant attention to and monitoring of the environment, hazards and potential dangers

8. Self awareness

9. Proper management of personal issues and impulses

10. Complete awareness that WE ARE NOT MIND READERS

The Driver's Mirror

ISSUES COMPROMISING A SAFE DRIVING EXPERIENCE

- A. Poor training and preparation for driving
- B. Acting-out behaviour(s)
- C. Impairment(s)
- D. Poor Judgment
- E. Limited insight into or concern for the psychology of the driving situation
- F. Limited insight into or concern about responsibilities and consequences

A. Poor Training and Preparation for Driving

There are various possibilities or reasons for this including:

- The driver does not have a driver's license nor has the driver had any official training, supervision or testing.

- The driver has used personal contacts, bribes, political and/or family influence or an unregulated licensing situation to acquire a driver's license, without proper training and preparation.

- The driver has gotten a friend or associate, with poor driving habits and attitudes, to teach him or her about driving and these bad habits are not observed or corrected by the licensing authority.

- The licensing authority does not properly educate the potential driver about all aspects of the driving situation **including the psychology of the driving situation**.

- The licensing authority does not properly test the potential driver in on-road situations and/or provides poorly-constructed written tests which do not adequately test the driver's knowledge, attitude or **psychological** preparedness.

The Driver's Mirror

Example.

A 10-year-old boy on a dare from friends, gets the keys to his father's manual truck and with his friends in the back, heads off downhill. His friends are yelling and jumping up and down, egging him on to go faster. One gets up on the roof of the cab, holding onto the door openings. At a T junction ahead, a large truck turns toward them. The underage driver will have to veer to avoid a collision and cannot reach the brake pedal. Several cars are parked on both sides of the road. Something bad will surely happen.

Example.

A young exchange student from foreign country asks a friend to teach him how to drive. The friend obliges, but the student does not realise the fellow has poor driving habits and has already attracted several traffic violations, tends to drive while texting friends, does not use his seatbelt and shows an inpatient contempt for older drivers.
The student is called home on a family emergency and cannot return to his studies.
The student tells his father that he now knows how to drive, so the father bribes a local official to get him his license.
The student is usually a nice person, but behind the wheel he has a superior and entitled attitude and the bad habits taught to him by his friend will have serious consequences for himself and others.

IDEALLY- A driver should only have the privilege of driving in public after reaching the mandated age and being properly instructed by an unbiased, objective professional instructor and a psychological assessor and/or counselor (who are accountable to accepted standards) and after passing comprehensive written and on-road evaluations and satisfying strict testing of psychological and physical status.

The Driver's Mirror

B. Acting-out Behaviour(s)

When a person puts a feeling, urge, impulse, emotion, belief, unresolved issue, objection, dissatisfaction, and/or desire into a behaviour or behaviours instead of into words via a statement, discussion or request, that person is **acting-out.**

Acting-out is usually considered to be a **maladaptive, negative strategy** which leads to **complications** in issues, relationships or circumstances. Acting-out is considered to be evidence of **emotional immaturity**, demonstrates **poor awareness of the consequences of one's behaviour** and shows a **basic lack of respect and sensitivity toward another person**. Acting-out also **compromises the personal image of the perpetrator**, reduces the respect, trust and consideration which that person receives from others and, in the case of driving behaviour, can lead to costly consequences.

Examples of acting-out

- Driving fast when angry
- Deliberately driving slowly in the 'fast' lane
- Honking horn unnecessarily
- Making rude hand gestures at others
- Impeding other drivers on purpose
- Aggressive tailgating in reaction to another driver's cautious behaviour
- Yelling at, verbally abusing or rudely gesturing at another driver

The Driver's Mirror

Example.

An angry man, who has just been fired for bullying workmates and has just beaten up his wife, storms off in his car. When he sees a man who looks like a foreigner, his road rage causes him to threaten and harass the other driver.

So focused is his rage, he fails to see a little girl crossing the highway and runs over her, killing her.

Realising what he has done, he takes off in high speed reckless abandon, intent on suicide. The likelihood of a further catastrophe is extremely high!

Indeed, he gets involved in a high-speed car chase with police, rams several vehicles and crashes through a roadblock, before being shot and wounded by a police sniper from a helicopter. He lives and faces many years of imprisonment.

IDEALLY- Whatever motivates acting-out should be dealt with at another time in a more adaptive manner, such as by talking about or discussing issues, conflicts, problems or feelings with a significant other and/or getting psychological or medical assistance, counseling, guidance or treatment.

C. Impairments

These could be due to

- Ill health - Allergy reactions - car exhaust, recently eaten food, perfumes

The Driver's Mirror

- Headaches, dizziness

- Low energy/poor concentration

- Nausea

- Driver in pain

- Epilepsy, cataplexy, narcolepsy, fainting and or lightheadedness

- Mental illness (see pages 23-25)

- Fatigue/tiredness/drowsiness

Example.

A truck driver, tired and driving too fast on a wet road, cannot negotiate a corner and crashes his truck into someone's house. The wall collapses, falls inward and kills two small children inside. The mother, dumbstruck and in shock, dissociates and becomes mute. The marriage falls apart because the husband cannot accept the loss, and turns to alcohol.
The house was not insured.
The driver's marriage also collapses, as his wife is enraged by his repeated irresponsibility. The driver's friends abandon him. He is charged and goes to prison, where he is raped and beaten by fellow prisoners.

The Driver's Mirror

- Poor hearing
  - Failure to acquire or maintain hearing aids
  - Driving with music turned up too loudly
  - Illegally wearing head phones while driving

- Poor vision/visibility
  - Failure to use visual aids
  - Failure to update visual aids
  - Problems with peripheral vision
  - Failure to repair wipers or use wipers at appropriate speeds
  - Failure to wash dirt, grease, grime from windows
  - Use of shades/tinting which block vision
  - Use of dark glasses at night
  - Driving into the sun without visor down or sunglasses on
  - Adornment of vehicle with items which might block visual field (flowers, stuffed animals, trinkets in back window or shiny items reflecting in the wind screen)
  - Transporting boxes, plants and/or other items which block the visual field
  - Not having or knowing how to use the rear view mirrors
  - Dirty or broken rearview mirrors
  - Cracks in windows which distort visual images

Example.

An elderly man who forgot his hearing aide, has also failed to update his glasses. He is arguing with his wife about taking a wrong turn. When someone runs across the road, he accidentally steps on the accelerator instead of the brake and strikes the person, who, severely injured, lays on the road. Flustered and in a panic, he rapidly drives off with his wife screaming and crying beside him. She refuses to ride with him again.

The Driver's Mirror

- Consumption of

    - Excess food or fluids
    - Alcoholic beverages
    - Drugs, both prescription and nonprescription

Example.

A driver has been using recreational drugs and/or alcohol and without realizing it suffers detrimental changes to judgment, decision-making, reaction times and/or perceptions and immediately endangers self and others when operating the vehicle. Even if not angry or with negative/troubled/conflicted thoughts, the drug's effects render the driver an impaired person. If the driver **is also** angry, upset, impulsive and/or has attitudinal problems, the risks are magnified and bad outcomes become even more likely. If the driver **is** an alcohol or drug-dependent person, he or she may **always** be impaired sufficiently to interfere with safe operation of a vehicle.

The Driver's Mirror

- Mental illness/abnormal mental states associated with illness

    - Depression (causes poor concentration and/or judgment, sluggish actions/decisions, distractibility, low energy, low motivation, uncaring attitude, memory problems, suicidal ideas and behaviours)

    - Mania (causes grandiosity, poor judgment, false perceptions of ability, excessive risk-taking)

    - Irritability (causes anger, poor judgment, impulsivity, acting-out)

    - Anxiety (causes nervousness, hesitation, indecisiveness, fear/apprehension)

    - Attention-deficit problems (cause distractibility, poor concentration)

    - Obsessive/compulsive problems (cause excessive checking or other repetitive, distracting behaviour(s))

    - Sleep disorders (cause drowsiness and risk of sleeping at the wheel)

    - Dementia (causes memory, concentration, judgment and decision-making compromises)

    - Psychosis/hallucinations (cause(s) perceptual distractions, problems with judgment, decision-making and reality testing)

    - Flashbacks (displaces the here-and-now while the person is reliving a past event)

The Driver's Mirror

- Intrusive thoughts (interfere with concentration)

- Dissociative episodes (altered state of awareness often with acting-out of repressed states or feelings or disconnection from the here-and-now)

- Personality disorders (associated with problem attitudes, anger, disrespect, acting-out, blaming, victim mentality and a host of other maladaptive beliefs and behaviours)

Example.

A woman with schizoaffective disorder has not been compliant with her usually-effective treatment medications, because of limited insight. She believes that criminals and police are conspiring to follow and rape her. While driving, she believes she recognizes undercover unmarked police cars, so she speeds up to weave in and out of traffic. She ignores stop signs and stoplights in her psychotic panic.

The Driver's Mirror

Her auditory hallucinations tell her to cause an accident to divert the police, so she can get away.

She rear ends an old woman's car, causing the old lady to lose control and sideswipe a car being driven by a teenage girl who is taking her younger brother to his piano lesson. Although these people manage to stop without sustaining injuries, the psychotic woman speeds on, still frightened for her life.
She decides to suicide to put an end to the harassment. She rams her car into a bridge abutment and sustains a severe head injury, broken ribs, fractured pelvis and bilateral fracture femurs. Her spleen is ruptured and after months of rehabilitation she can barely walk, is now resistant to antipsychotic medications and becomes addicted to pain medication.

- Problems with time perception
  (how long it will take to slow/stop or speed up to accomplish a maneuver)

- Problems with distance perception
  (distance between vehicles, for example)

- Problems with speed perception
  (misjudging of distance to stop the vehicle)

IDEALLY- A person refrains from driving when he or she is aware of any impairments or states of mind or emotions which could affect safe operation of the vehicle and his or her ability to properly react to or manage the complexities of driving, including reacting appropriately to traffic delays or road obstructions. A person uses necessary visual or hearing aids and properly prepares the vehicle for safe operation with unobstructed vision and proper containment of passengers, animals and potential projectiles.

The Driver's Mirror

D. Poor Judgment

Judgment could be impaired or compromised because of

- Intelligence quotient
- Emotional issues
    - Anger, anxiety, emotional distress, grief, depression, fear, irritability

- Psychological issues
    - Narcissism
    - Low self-esteem
    - Lack of assertiveness
    - Aggressiveness, arrogance, sense of entitlement
    - Paranoia
    - Over-concern for others
    - Under-concern for others
    - Overconfidence
    - Indecisiveness
    - Fear and/or anxiety
    - Projection of issues onto others
    - Denial of wrong doing/responsibility/ accountability
    - Rationalisation of actions
    - Inappropriate competitiveness

The Driver's Mirror

Example.

A young fellow adorns his car with racing stripes, loud mufflers, slogans and aggressive stickers.
Even before he gets into the vehicle to drive, his mindset is to go as fast as possible. He finds other drivers an obstacle and acts aggressively toward them. He is not courteous, is easily angered and cuts in and out of traffic, using his horn inappropriately and making rude hand gestures to other drivers. He has a contemptuous attitude toward anyone over 30 years of age. He behaves as if driving is a video game! He is an accident waiting to happen.

- Certain beliefs

    - Invulnerability, "I will not have an accident"
    - Entitlement, for example, "I can do whatever I want/I have a drivers license/I am important/I am wealthy/I have a better car"

-"Other vehicles are just obstacles"
-"Other drivers are out to get me"
-"I should be able to drive as fast as I want"
-"Nothing will happen to me because I am a good driver"

The Driver's Mirror

- "If something happens it will be someone else's fault"
- "I am being followed"
- "Someone is after me"
- Misplaced trust in the mechanical integrity of the vehicle and tyres
- The end justifies the means, for example: "Because I have to go so far by 6 o'clock, I can drive fast and go around slow drivers."

Example.

The only water buffalo of a poor family is killed on the road by the reckless son of a local businessman, who bribes police to avoid charges. The family used the beloved animal for transportation, milk, pulling the wagon and plowing the fields. They are financially devastated.

When the father goes to the local businessman to seek compensation, he is severely beaten by the businessman's employees and told to keep his mouth shut.

Although the wife urges him to drop the issue, the farmer seeks vengeance on the businessman's son and kills him. He is imprisoned and later killed and the businessman goes to court, has the family's property confiscated and the family evicted.

The mother has to place her children with relatives and becomes a domestic worker to survive.

The Driver's Mirror

- Dementing illness

    - Forgetting destination
    - Confusion about the operation of vehicle
    - Forgetting road rules
    - Misperception of distance
    - Misperception of speed

- Mental illness (See pages 23-25)

- Poor driver education (See page 16, 17)

- Acting contrary to one's better judgment and/or rationalizing one's driving behaviour(s)

- Engaging in distracting activities while driving

    - Eating
    - Smoking
    - Reading
    - Applying makeup
    - Adjusting hair/shaving

The Driver's Mirror

- Adjusting clothing
- Using/adjusting a cellular/mobile telephone or other electronic or entertainment device
- Thinking about other issues other than driving
- 'Gawking' at roadside events
- Turning around in seat to talk to someone in the back or front seat
- Dealing with children/pets in a moving vehicle
- Engaging in sexual behavior
- Using or attempting to use a urine-collection container while driving
- Ear/teeth/face/fingernail cleaning
- Nose-picking or eyelash-plucking

Example.

Four teenage girlfriends are driving in a convertible, out for a good time. They are driving too fast on a mountain road, are singing and whistling at guys they pass. The driver is applying lipstick, smoking and showing off by weaving back and forth across the lanes. If an animal runs out in front of them, it is unlikely that she will react in time. An accident is highly likely.

The Driver's Mirror

- Failure to get off the road to use toilet facilities and thus being distracted and distressed

IDEALLY - A person recognises and appropriately takes into account his or her biases, prejudices, compromises and/or emotional issues, so that his or her driving behaviour still conforms to all safety, legal, respectful and courtesy expectations. If the person realises his or her judgment is sufficiently impaired to cause undue risk, he or she refrains from driving. The driver does not allow distractions and does not engage in any activity other than total concentration on the safe operation of vehicle.

E. Limited Insight Into or Concern for the Psychology of the Driving Situation

Quite possibly, only a minority of drivers are aware of their own psychology as they operate their vehicle. That is, aware of

- what is motivating them at any particular period of time to engage in their style of thinking and their behaviour

- their feelings, the sources of the feelings and how they should manage those feelings

The Driver's Mirror

- whether they are reacting rationally or irrationally to their impulses, prejudices, fears, anxieties, frustrations, conflicts and internal issues

- how the way they are managing their issues, expectations, impatience, pressures, internal and external distractions, can affect their safety, the safety of others and the manner in which they operate their vehicle

Certain drivers, in certain mental/physical states, appear to be taking excessive risks or are in denial regarding risks and often do not appear to be concerned for their own safety nor the safety of others nor whether they obey the road rules, drive according to the road conditions, drive according to their own medical status or drive to stay alive!

Drivers who are:

- Tired and drowsy
- Depressed or suicidal
- Angry, irritable or homicidal
- Psychotic
- Chemically-impaired
- Driving without needed visual or hearing aids
- Grief-stricken
- Driving with severe or panic anxiety

The Driver's Mirror

- In severe pain from headaches or other severe pathology

- Experiencing acute medical emergencies/situations, such as bleeding, giving birth, having severe chest or respiratory distress, retinal detachment or other compromising problems

IDEALLY- The driver becomes increasingly self-aware and increasingly able to deal with unresolved, worrisome, personal and/or interpersonal issues through reflection, reading, observations, psychotherapy and/or accepting feedback from others and is able to recognize his or her emotional and mental status prior to and while operating the vehicle, in order to minimize projections, adverse behaviours, the likelihood of acting out and/or becoming entrained into the behaviours of problem drivers. The driver declines to drive when he or she realizes some compromise could affect performance and safety. The driver becomes less reactive and more thoughtful in all circumstances.

The Driver's Mirror

F. Limited Insight Into or Concern About Responsibilities and Consequences

- Poor driver education (see pages 16, 17)

- Driver from out of jurisdiction unfamiliar with road rules

- Inexperienced drivers

- Under-age drivers

- Drivers with impaired mental states (see pages 19, 20, 22-29)

    - Intellectual impairment
    - Psychotic or mentally ill drivers
    - Dementing drivers

- Drivers with personality and/or attitudinal problems and/or antisocial tendencies
  Example.

The Driver's Mirror

If a driver who was **not** abusing addictive substances or sedative prescribed medications operates the vehicle while impaired in some **other** way, the chance of a mishap increases with each additional compromising issue.

For example, if a young angry pregnant mother is tired and emotionally upset, has smudged glasses, a dirty windscreen, is not wearing sunglasses while driving into the sun, has a viral illness, is on benzodiazepines for anxiety(can cause drowsiness) , has crying children in the car and has one or more soft tyres or broken side mirrors, a disaster is likely. This person should not be driving and should either get a taxi, use public transportation or ask a responsible relative or friend to assist.

IDEALLY- The driver realises the responsibility to be properly prepared and informed, to operate a properly maintained vehicle, to drive according to the prevailing weather and traffic circumstances, in an amenable frame of mind, in a stable and alert physical state and realises the consequences of making any compromises and engaging in any illegal, irresponsible, aggressive, careless or destructive behaviours which could result in loss of life and limb.
An insightful driver realises that there are other drivers and passengers in other vehicles who are vulnerable and in need of protection such as children, the elderly and pregnant women and drives to ensure everyone's safety.

The driver familiarizes himself/herself with local road rules, signage and laws prior to driving in a new jurisdiction.

The Driver's Mirror

Common Causes of Avoidable Mishaps and Associated Psychology

Of all the above issues which can compromise the driving experience, the **most common** causes of vehicular mishaps, **completely within the control of the driver**, include:

- allowing distractions to compromise safety (including gawking, sticky-beaking, rubbernecking)
- driver tiredness, drowsiness or fatigue (postprandial, after taxing physical or mental work or related to driving between 2300 and 800 hours)
- driving while intoxicated from misuse of alcohol, medications or drugs of abuse
- driving too fast for the conditions or to safely react to potential or unexpected dangers or circumstances
- driving aggressively and endangering self and others or being subjected to the dangerous behaviours of an aggressive driver and either becoming entrained into the behaviour or reacting in a manner which does not decrease risks
- failing to maintain the vehicle and to carry emergency equipment to use in response to adverse weather or breakdown conditions
- driving without a seatbelt or with a damaged/faulty seatbelt and/or failing to insist that passengers use seatbelts and/or failing to provide appropriate safety seats or restraining devices for children.

Remember that anything not fastened down in the vehicle becomes a projectile in an accident!

The Driver's Mirror

Common Reasons or Psychological Issues Influencing the Above Behaviours

- Denial, "It will not happen to me"
- Poor Judgment, "Even though I am tired/drunk/hung-over/angry, I can still drive safely."
- Defiance, "No one can tell me what to do!"
- Grandiosity, "My driving is so good, I will not have an accident."
  "I have good reflexes and can react quickly to whatever happens."
  "I can multitask."
- Projection, "If everyone else does what **they** are supposed to do, there will be no problem."
- Rationalization, "Only bad drivers have accidents."
- Misplaced priorities, "I am more comfortable without my seatbelt on."
- Uncaring, "Even if something happens, so what."
- Fatalism, "If it is meant to be, there is nothing I can do about it."
- Poor appreciation of consequences, "I never thought something like that would happen."
- Preoccupation, "I was rushing to the hospital after I heard my wife was in an accident and forgot to wear my seatbelt."
- Mismanaged anger, "If the other pricks would just get off the road, everything would be fine."
- Entitlement, "I can do whatever I want."
- Mistaken beliefs, "I have rights."
- Poorly informed, "I did not know I had to wear a seatbelt."

The Driver's Mirror

The Psychology of Speeding

Although a driver may disagree with the posted speed limit, it is better for that driver to submit a written challenge to the local governmental jurisdiction for a review of the situation, rather than to arbitrarily decide on a speed which is faster than the posted limit, as in doing so, the driver is driving illegally. Many factors must be taken into account by authorities when deciding on local speed limits.

In some jurisdictions speed limits are recommended and not absolute, but a prudent, mature driver will always appropriately adapt the vehicle speed to the weather, topographic or traffic conditions and in response to the requirements of the law.

Although there are drivers who periodically or regularly drive **below** the speed limits due to

- inexperience
- timidity
- fear or apprehension
- anxiety problems
- distractions
- age or infirmity

the most common moving violation is that of **exceeding** the speed limit. This is referred to as **speeding.**

The Driver's Mirror

Common Reasons for or Psychological Issues Associated with Speeding

- time pressures associated with a busy personal or work schedule

- failure to plan ahead or for conditions, with consequent feeling of pressure and rushing

- impulsiveness and thrill-seeking

- feelings of entitlement or self-indulgence

- the addictive nature of speed

- impatience and/or acting-out due to disagreement with speed restrictions

- defiance and mismanagement of anger and contempt for rules

- disdain for compliant, law-abiding drivers

- risk-taking lifestyle

- risk-taking game with police or gambling against the odds

- grandiose appraisal of ability or of the capacities of the vehicle

- purchase of a vehicle with power in excess of that required in actual speed-limit conditions

- being influenced by vehicle advertisements showing speeding in various unrealistic conditions

- succumbing to enticing advertisements showing speeding as a fun, challenging, or status activity

- the rationalized association between speeding and 'freedom' or one's 'rights'

The Driver's Mirror

- a demonstration of poor judgment/acting-out/poor awareness of consequences, when speeding in hazardous conditions

- a reflection of distorted perception of ability and safety when the driver is under the influence of alcohol/substances/medications/pain/fatigue

- ignorance regarding or denial of the physics of speed and risks in unexpected situations

- rationalized by the example of other lawbreakers or to evade another lawbreaker (tailgater)

- needing to get somewhere quickly, such as to the toilet/hospital/home for an emergency

- an opportunity to try to manipulate a police officer with wit, charm or fantastic excuses

- a calculated activity with acceptance of consequences in a risk/benefit analysis

- justified by the driver because the police frequently exceed the speed limit!

Behaviours and Psychological Issues Associated with Being Caught

Although many of the behaviours and issues which compromise a safe driving experience are worrisome, but not in themselves illegal, others **are** definitely illegal and attract legal penalties or consequences.

Some examples include, leaving the scene of an accident, parking in restricted areas (such as in front of fire hydrants), failure to pay parking fees, speeding, driving under the influence of alcohol and drugs, driving without a valid license, driving while under suspension, reckless driving, speeding in a

The Driver's Mirror

school zone during specified hours, ignoring an occupied pedestrian crosswalk, driving in the wrong direction in a traffic lane, use of a vehicle to damage or destroy property or to endanger people or animals, speeding through yellow/red lights, and/or various other illegal activities.

Some drivers, believing they have 'rights', interpret this as permission to do whatever they wish, until caught and knowingly/deliberately break the law. How antisocial ! Others break the law due to absent-mindedness, distractions, lack of concentration, preoccupation, poor judgment, acting-out or due to other compromises. **This does not excuse them from the consequences**, as they should not have been driving if they were not prepared to accept responsibilities and fully attend to this complex activity and should have noted and properly responded to, regulatory signs and specific circumstances (such as parking restrictions).

Although serious psychological problems are often associated with the commission of offenses, the manner in which a driver reacts **when caught** committing an illegal act, can also reveal a disturbed personal psychology, attitude or philosophy. It is not uncommon, for example, for a parking warden, a policeman or policewoman, a highway patrolman, a motorcycle policeman or other regulatory official to be blamed by the perpetrator as the cause of the problem!

Excuses are more common than acceptance of consequences !

The Driver's Mirror

The following are some of behaviours and psychological issues associated with being caught after the commission of an offense.

- Acting bewildered, "Why are you arresting me/giving me a violation ticket?"
- Denial, "I didn't do anything wrong." "It's not my fault."
- Making excuses, "But I am late for work." "I wasn't speeding any faster than anyone else."
- Contritely apologizing, "I am terribly sorry officer, I don't know what I was thinking!"
- Pleading for no consequences, "Oh please officer, how could you ruin my record?!"
- Verbalizing lies, "But the speedometer said 100 KPH" (the needle just touched the right side of the 100 but was beyond the actual 100 mark on the speedometer)
- Drunken or inebriated ramblings or ravings, "You useless pig. Why aren't you catching rapists or home screwing your Mrs.?"
- Verbal abuse directed toward the officer, "You motherf---ing asshole useless son of a bitch."
- Physical aggression, threats or assaults, with or without weapons
- Psychotic rambling or confession, "Are you with the CIA? They have been following me for the last hour and have planted microphones in my car. I can't seem to shake them."
- Bribery, "Are you sure I can't do something for you or give you something to change your mind?"
- Bargaining, "I contributed to the police fund and will again, if you don't issue a ticket."
- Indifference, "Go ahead officer, do what you have to do, I don't care."
- Defiance, "I will take this to court and beat it and tie you up with paperwork."
- Indignation and arrogance, "You petty government functionaries don't have anything better to do."
- Speeding from the scene in an attempt to evade consequences

The Driver's Mirror

- Tearing up the ticket and throwing it on the ground
- Deliberately failing to pay the fine
- Repeating the same offense with little caring about consequences
- Making halfhearted promises to a judge/policeman to evade or lessen consequences

Driving is a social privilege to which is attached many responsibilities and obligations.

Due to the fact that every person who possesses a valid driver's license is supposed to have studied the traffic laws in the jurisdiction and is obligated to fully understand what is legal, proper, courteous, civilized driving-behaviour and what is illegal, dangerous, offensive, discourteous, compromising driving-behaviour, there is **no** excuse for a driver to claim ignorance or to expect exceptions or immunity (diplomatic personnel perhaps being the only ostensible exception) or to put his or her psychological/personal issues over issues of safety and compliance with the law. It is also a reflection of a misguided attitude or philosophy for the driver to see the driving experience as a game or competition between him or herself and other drivers and/or the regulatory authorities.

The Psychology of Risk-Taking Behaviour

Whether through procrastination, neglect, poor insight into consequences, denial or another reason, a driver may fail to regularly assure the proper maintenance of the vehicle, so that the tyres and mechanical/electrical systems may not be sound and roadworthy.

A driver may regularly/periodically speed, evade parking fees, tailgate, change lanes or position without using indicators, drive without headlights activated, straddle lanes, speed close to parked cars/people/animals, engage in discourteous, antisocial or dangerous driving-behaviours, drive under the influence of alcohol or drugs, drive without a valid license or while the license is suspended or engage in other deliberate risk-taking behaviours, all the while operating under the mistaken

The Driver's Mirror

assumption that because he or she has not been caught yet, he or she can continue to act-out or to engage in those behaviours. There may be many reasons, some psychological, for this risk-taking approach to driving. These include,

- false economy
- grandiosity/arrogance
- denial/minimisation/rationalisation
- defiance
- mismanaged anger/frustration/feelings/conflicts
- selfishness
- poor judgment
- uncaring/indifference
- contempt for others/laws/regulations/rules/control/limits
- impulsiveness

Knowingly engaging in any risk-taking behaviour reflects a very maladaptive, if not antisocial, attitude about safety issues, obligations, rights, duties and responsibilities, as a co-user of a public facility.

A mature, prudent driver minimizes all known risks, is always aware of consequences, drives in such a way as to ensure safety and adherence to social and legal requirements, takes the responsibilities of driving seriously and has an appreciative, sharing approach to the privilege of driving.

Problem Drivers with Psychological Issues

The following are just a few of the many drivers who reveal psychological issues and problem or compromising behaviours in the course of driving. Some of these drivers have **serious psychological problems** and persist in acting-out or behaving in ways which endanger themselves and others.

The Driver's Mirror

Such drivers are encouraged to seek psychological help and refrain from acting-out their many issues in the driving arena.

Excessively Cautious or Timid Drivers

- leave large gaps in front of their vehicles into which other drivers keep intruding
- go slower than other traffic or than the road conditions allow, within the speed limit
- impede the flow of traffic
- cause dangerous situations, as other drivers compensate for them
- become the catalyst for further problem behaviours in impatient, competitive or aggressive drivers

Curiosity Seekers/Gawkers

- increase the risk of accidents for themselves and others by concentrating on something other than driving
- impede the flow of traffic
- become the catalyst for further problem behaviours in impatient, competitive or aggressive drivers

'Follower' Drivers

- choose to drive behind another driver or other drivers and may or may not tailgate

The Driver's Mirror

'Herd' Drivers

- drive **not** in relation to the speed limit, highway rules or conditions but in reaction to other drivers, by grouping together with other drivers, instead of spreading out for safety (especially in conditions of rain, snow or fog)

'Leader' Drivers

- attempt to stay out in front of other vehicles, even by engaging in speeding and/or maneuvering behaviours
- may focus so much on being ahead of others, that other conditions or dangers are not appreciated
- may pass one group of vehicles, speed through the gap, then attempt to pass the next group.

Aggressive/Impatient/Competitive Drivers

- demonstrate little tolerance or courtesy for other drivers, whom they see as an impediment
- tailgate in an aggressive or intimidating manner
- drive into restricted lanes or off the pavement to pass others
- flash lights and/or sound horn unnecessarily
- make aggressive eye contact or gestures to provoke others to yield, compete or race
- arrogant or entitled behaviours

'Policeman' Drivers

- adopt passive-resistance behaviours to regulate the speed or movement of other drivers
- make critical faces or disapproving gestures toward problem drivers

The Driver's Mirror

Problem Heavy-Vehicle and Truck Drivers

- obstruct the flow of the 'fast' lane
- tailgate dangerously
- use the size and mass of the vehicle to push into or block traffic
- drive the truck like a car
- pass another vehicle in a tardy manner, thereby obstructing traffic

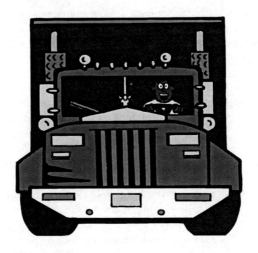

Inconsiderate Drivers

- show no consideration for or courtesy to other drivers, including truck drivers
- refuse to allow another vehicle to merge in preparation for the off ramp or at a converging-traffic situation, for example

'Oblivious' Drivers

- drive as if unaware of almost everything around them, including pedestrians, cyclists, other drivers, large vehicles, speed limit signs and /or obstructions

The Driver's Mirror

'Road Ragers'

Of all the drivers on the road, the ones who are the most troubled, traumatizing, dangerous and potentially lethal toward other drivers, are those who engage in 'road rage'.

Such drivers reveal very worrisome problems in one or more of the areas which could compromise safe driving (see pages 15-34)

The following are some are the many factors which could predispose to this type of extreme, dangerous, offensive behaviour, **BUT ARE NOT EXCUSABLE IN THE CONTEXT OF DRIVING**

- inherited or acquired neurological damage or illnesses which could result in poor impulse control, impaired judgment, irritability, explosive anger, abnormal perceptions of others and/or difficulties with decision-making
- a history of personal, physical, emotional, sexual, spiritual abuse, neglect or mistreatment
- a history of other types of antisocial behaviours such as killing animals, setting fires, destruction of property, fighting, bullying, intimidating or engaging in aggressive behaviours toward others
- a history of poor coping and emotional management, especially with regard to accumulated stressors, frustrations and anger
- substance-use-related disinhibition
- mental-illness-related states of mind, including paranoia, grandiosity, rage, moodiness and/or irritability
- personality disorder with a history of impatience, intolerance, inconsiderate behaviours, selfishness, acting-out, an entitled attitude or other pathological uncaring, dismissive, disrespectful, belittling or antisocial attitude
- not caring about responsibilities and/or consequences

The Driver's Mirror

'Road rage' behaviours can include

- violent yelling, swearing or screaming at or verbally threatening, insulting, mocking, racially-abusing another driver
- aggressive gestures and body language directed toward another driver
- attempting to run into or actually running into other driver's vehicle, forcing it off the road or blocking its progress
- aggressive tailgating, with or without horn blowing
- forcing another driver to stop and then engaging in physical attacks on the driver, driver's vehicle or passengers, either with fists, feet or implements/ weapons, sometimes with intent to kill
- intimidating, aggressive following with the intent to frighten, punish and or harm the other driver
- throwing objects at or shooting at the other driver or driver's vehicle

Any driver prone to 'road rage' is urged to seek professional assistance as soon as possible and to postpone driving.

The Driver's Mirror

Interactions with Other Drivers

Driving is a social experience and the driver interacts with other drivers at all times.

The driver can react to another driver's **objective** cues, signals and/or behaviours, such as gestures, smiles, frowns, angry looks, puzzled looks, mouthed words or voiced words and can engage in positive or negative behaviours or responses. The driver may misinterpret these cues, signals or behaviours and/or ignore them.

But the driver can also **project** his or her own issues, beliefs, moods, urges, prejudices and/or expectations into the interaction and because of this, may become convinced, **usually quite incorrectly**, that he or she knows what the other driver intends to do or not do, what is in the other driver's mind and/or intentions, and/or what the other driver may think or feel about him or her!

In reaction to the other driver(s), the driver:

- **can set up positive or negative interactions with the other driver(s)**
- **can be influenced by the cues, signals and/or behaviours of the other driver(s)**
- **can become entrained into positive or negative driving behaviours**
- **can be neutral and look for more information (the healthy, mature alternative)**

Social or antisocial driving reactions and behaviours can result. Problem driving and/or problem, negative interactions, for any reason, increase(s) the likelihood of mishaps.

The Driver's Mirror

Illustrative examples.

An older woman is driving very slowly and cautiously. A younger driver behind her becomes impatient, cuts out in front of an approaching vehicle and speeds past her, giving her a nasty look.

The approaching driver blows the horn and gestures rudely at the younger driver. The older woman, puzzled and frightened by all of this, pulls to the side of the road and is very reluctant to continue.

A young fellow is stopped at a stoplight, when another guy in a 'muscle car' pulls up beside him and revs his engine. Interpreting this as a challenge, he gestures to the other driver and when the light turns green, they speed off in a race. They weave in and out of traffic at high speed. Soon several other aggressive males join in. A multi-car pileup ensues, followed by fights and threats.

An impatient young woman is trying to drive very quickly in heavy traffic, dangerously tailgates the vehicle in front of her and makes rude hand gestures toward the driver. She manages to intrude into the neighboring lane, where she continues this behaviour. When the driver of the car she was tailgating exits at the next off-ramp, there she is, only one car ahead and still impatient!

A driver sees a gesture from a driver to the right and kindly slows to allow that car to go ahead first. The second driver waves and offers a courtesy to yet another driver. The driver who initiated the courtesy reaches work and is surprised to discover that the recipient of the courtesy is the new boss. Now **that** is a good first impression!

The Driver's Mirror

An angry man interprets the look of a male driver from another culture as a threat and starts hurling racial abuse at him. The other driver, fed up with this frequent behaviour, rams the angry man's car and gets out with a baseball bat, smashes his windows and assaults the angry driver, breaking his legs. Other drivers witnessing this, report to police that the man with the baseball bat started the incident.

The reactions and/or behaviours of ONE driver can have a significant ripple effect through traffic and on the reactions and/or behaviours of other drivers. A driver's decisions and behaviour can be very different between a low-traffic-volume and a high-traffic-volume situation. However, GOOD DRIVING IS JUST THAT, NO MATTER WHAT THE CIRCUMSTANCES

Traffic Games

There are drivers who, for various psychological reasons, seek to amuse themselves by interacting with other drivers in deliberate attempts to provoke those drivers into revealing impatience, poor impulse control, distractibility, gullibility or illegal behaviours.

This could give the provocative driver a sense of power and control over others, confirm his or her sense of superiority, reveal his or her antisocial tendencies or disrespect for safety or reveal other maladaptive personal problems.
The provocative driver may fail to appreciate the consequences of his or her actions, as the other driver, perhaps feeling that his or her weaknesses have been exposed or feeling humiliated, manipulated, provoked, embarrassed or mocked, could potentially seek retribution or act-out in some aggressive or dangerous manner.

The following are several examples of traffic 'games' in which the psychological issues of the provocateur and the other driver could interact in potentially very negative ways.

The Driver's Mirror

- The provocateur pretends to want to race, either from a standstill or while in motion. He or she, through eye contact, facial expressions, gestures, words or engine revving, seeks to challenge the other driver to a race. However the provocateur does **not** race and laughs at the gullibility of the other driver, who races off, breaking the speed laws.

- The provocateur deliberately slows down to prevent the follower-driver from being able to legally cross an intersection. The follower-driver must stop for the red light.
  Had the provocateur not done this, the other driver would have had sufficient time to also go through the intersection.

- The provocateur of one gender behaves in such a way as to provoke or tease the driver of the opposite gender. For example a female driver flashes her smiles, bats her eyelashes, throws pretend kisses, exposes a breast or engages in other provocative behaviours toward a male driver, to see his reaction and to gauge the magnitude of the effect she can have on him and his behaviour. When he responds, she may continue to distract him or completely ignore him to frustrate and confuse him.

- A driver allows or encourages his or her passenger(s) to engage in various games such as 'mooning', playing 'LIS' (Let It Show)(exposing sexual parts) or making rude, threatening or aggressive gestures toward another targeted driver to distract, entertain, or provoke him or her.

- The provocateur, who **usually** may **exceed** the speed limit, drives at or under the speed limit to frustrate an obviously impatient follower-driver, provoking that person to pass or to reveal his or her impatience or poor impulse control. The provocateur's smiles, smirks or laughs may further provoke the other driver.

The Driver's Mirror

- Two drivers collude with each other to block following traffic. They may want to see how far they can go before the follower-drivers engage in countermeasures such as tailgating, light-flashing, horn-blowing or attempting to drive around them or resist responding to these countermeasures.

- The provocative driver deliberately plays 'chicken' by heading straight for an oncoming driver.

A mature driver with good impulse control, safety-awareness, concentration and law-abiding attitude, will not get entrained into the games or strategies of another driver who attempts to manipulate, provoke, play with or endanger him or her.

Defensive Driving

Various factors determine whether a driver's driving style is, for example, reactive, aggressive, oblivious, apprehensive or defensive:

- the driver's psychological issues and/or problems, including any tendency, for example, to minimization, denial, acting-out or projection of responsibility onto others

The Driver's Mirror

- the driver's skill level and level of confidence
- the driver's judgment
- the driver's awareness of consequences
- the driver's ability to perceive options and dangers
- the way in which the driver is managing emotional and other distracting issues

A **reactive** driver tends not to plan ahead or to survey the traffic situation for possible problems and dangers, but merely reacts when something happens.

An **aggressive** driver drives as if others are an impediment and uses speed, intimidation and intrusive behaviours to selfishly act-out in traffic.

An **oblivious** driver seems not to be aware of anything happening around him or her, is not planning ahead and may not even be prepared to react to a situation.

An **apprehensive** driver fears problems and as a result drives in an overly cautious, timid, nonassertive or hesitant manner, which could **cause** problem situations.

The driving style most likely to be associated with a good driving outcome, is described as DEFENSIVE.

A defensive approach to driving is not a paranoid mind set. On the contrary it is a mindset where all conditions, options, risks, dangers, avenues for safety and potential compromises are in the driver's awareness and planning.

The Driver's Mirror

It is not just the unpredictable/predictable behaviour of another driver which is of interest to a defensive driver, but any and all factors which could cause risks or dangers or lead to potential mishaps.

A prudent driver is on the defense against, among other things,

- ignorance of local traffic laws and customs
- the way in which weather and road conditions can affect safety
- the effects of fatigue, malaise, jet lag, drowsiness, pain, emotion or physical discomfort
- having a full bladder or having to defecate
- distractions
- the potential of an animal, child, or other person/vehicle to unexpectedly enter the roadway
- the potential antisocial behaviors of others
- the possibility of a tyre blowout at any time
- another driver under the influence of drugs, alcohol or other impairment(s), as determined by the manner in which he/she is operating his/her vehicle

The following are some examples of the defensive strategies used by good drivers

- scanning ahead, to the sides and behind, using rearview mirrors, to constantly monitor activity in the driving environment
- closely observing the speed and direction of other drivers and anticipation of sudden and unpredictable behaviour on their part
- keeping the recommended distance from the driver in front to avoid collisions in sudden-stopping situations
- slowing down rather than speeding up if another car cuts in on an angle to get ahead of one's vehicle
- keeping one's distance from an erratic driver
- keeping distance from parked cars to avoid sudden door-opening and if in inside lane in two-forward-lane situation, matching outside lane's vehicle's avoidance-manoeuvre

The Driver's Mirror

- on winding roads, staying in one's lane rather than cutting corners, to avoid a collision with a rapidly-advancing oncoming vehicle
- obeying the official markings on the road and road signs
- in one-forward-lane situation keeping to the outside of the lane
- in a two-forward-lane situation, without a middle barrier/median, in the outside lane keeping to the outside and in the inside lane keeping to the middle of the lane. In a middle barrier/median situation, driving in the inside lane, keeping close to the barrier/median
- in a three-or-more-forward lane situation, driving in the outside and inside lanes as immediately above and in the middle lanes keeping to the middle of the lane
- activating headlights at all times
- using signal lights for every move
- in certain jurisdictions, driving under the assumption that every other driver is under the influence of drugs or alcohol or has attitude problems, until proven otherwise
- always locking the vehicle doors when operating and not operating the vehicle, even at gas/petrol stations, to avoid unauthorized entry of a person into the vehicle or theft of the vehicle or contents
- removing personal items, sound equipment, GPS systems, out of the vehicle to avoid break-ins
- making sure the vehicle is properly maintained and serviced
- being aware of, honest about and showing good judgment and management of compromises which could affect performance
- maintaining appropriate distances between one's vehicle and large vehicles, such as trucks
- keeping on the lookout for motorcyclists who could approach at speed, from any direction, at any time
- keeping one's distance and being cautious around farm animals, beasts of burden and farm equipment
- obeying all emergency and regulatory personnel

The Driver's Mirror

- using maps and GPS systems responsibly to navigate and stopping to get specific directions rather than engaging in distracting, exploratory driving
- if transporting objects, arranging them in such a manner as to not obstruct vision
- making sure all passengers are seated and secured with seatbelts or safety seats
- wearing sunglasses to reduce glare and eyestrain in sunny circumstances and properly using visors
- if one must drive in fog or blowing snow, using low beams or fog lights
- staying out of another driver's 'blind spot' , so as to be seen and being aware of own 'blind spot'
- child-proofing the vehicle for the safety of children

Any driver who does not accept the reasons and beneficial consequences of these defensive driving strategies, is thereby revealing that he or she has problems with judgment, attitude or personal psychology and **should not be driving**, until making the necessary readjustments to knowledge, attitude, self-management or driving philosophy.

When driving defensively, the life you save may be your own !

Antisocial Plotting/Colluding

The most common example of collusion with or facilitation of another driver's illegal behaviour occurs when a driver flashes his/her lights at an oncoming, speeding vehicle to warn that driver of a police speed trap. If the oncoming driver, prone to speeding, is later involved in a vehicular mishap or accident, the person who colluded with or facilitated his/her illegal behaviour is co-responsible for the outcome.

Truck drivers and other drivers can collude to block and impede traffic.

The Driver's Mirror

Not only do some drivers take unnecessary risks by using their mobile telephone/cell phone or engaging in 'texting' while driving, but also some particularly irresponsible, antisocial, self-centered drivers use their personal electronic devices and/or the Internet to inform other drivers of the locations of speed cameras/police speed-monitoring or of the locations of police breath-testing operations or to seek out such information from other sociopathic individuals.

Engaging in these types of behaviours demonstrates that the individuals concerned

- are showing contempt for the welfare of fellow citizens and for laws and safety
- are demonstrating worrisome lack of insight into or caring about the consequences of facilitating potential vehicular mishaps or accidents
- are revealing arrogance, selfishness, defiance, misplaced competitiveness with police and/or extremely poor judgment, in an attempt to evade the consequences of speeding or driving under the influence of alcohol or addictive substances
- are so focused on their own maladaptive issues and momentary needs, as to ignore their true social responsibilities and obligations
- do not see driving as a privilege but as a game
- are revealing serious psychological problems and/or pathological attitudes and values
- are potentially dangerous individuals capable of any other illegal, impulsive activity

The Driver's Mirror

Example.

A young woman in her 20s and her friends find it exciting and adventurous to attend parties on the weekend for the express purpose of getting drunk and 'high' on excessive amounts of alcohol and drugs. Prior to leaving the parties, the least-impaired friend checks Internet sources for information about the location of police monitoring, so the driver, always under the influence, can minimize the risk of being caught.
They think this is clever.
On one particular night, the group finds out that there is police 'booze bus' on a particular street, and so they avoid that location. Setting out thinking that they have gotten away with something, the driver, overconfident and impaired, speeds recklessly, loses control of the vehicle and runs head-on into another vehicle.
How clever is that ?!
The driver suffers a severe head injury and becomes quadriplegic, two of the friends in the front seat are killed, and the young woman and another friend in the back seat are badly shaken up.
The young woman is horrified when she learns that the deceased victims in the other car were her aunt and uncle, who were on their way home from a concert. Their small children are now parentless and the whole family is wracked with grief. How is she going to live with this ?!

Other examples of antisocial plotting include, planning on an illegal car race on a public street, vehicle vandalism or car theft, two drivers arranging another driver's accident or terrorists plotting a car/vehicle bombing.

Please think about what you are doing and about the potential consequences AT ALL TIMES !

The Driver's Mirror

Psychological & Physical Consequences of Problem Driving

Psychological aspects of the driving situation go far beyond those determining/affecting the behaviour/attitude of the driver.

Although accidents can happen even when alert, responsible, non-acting-out drivers are at the wheel, too many accidents can be avoided and are caused by any one or more driver problems, issues, compromises, inexperience, poor judgment or negative attitudes.

A mishap caused by a problem driver or situation can potentially have serious **physical** consequences for any of the following

- the driver
- the driver's passenger or passengers
- pets and animals in the vehicle
- another driver or other drivers
- the other driver's passenger or passengers
- pedestrian victim(s)
- animal victim(s)

The **physical** consequences can include

- death
- disfigurement, including facial injuries, loss of limb(s)
- head injuries and associated functional/intellectual/psychiatric impairments
- damage to or loss of vision
- neurological damage including paralysis, damage to hearing, development of periodic or constant dizziness, ataxia or unsteadiness
- damaged to or ruptured organs
- internal bleeding
- broken bones, including pelvis with possible consequences on reproductive capacity

The Driver's Mirror

- neck injuries with damage to voice, airway or swallowing mechanism
- other potential injuries

Any substantial or serious **physical injury** to any person or valued animal will usually be associated with temporary or permanent deformity, disability, impairments or loss of function, pain syndromes, the need for rehabilitation or the temporary or permanent consequences of loss of job, relationship(s), status, role functioning, self-esteem and self-respect or in other compromises.

Any substantial injury/damage to any person, valued animal or object, will always be associated with **psychological** distress and consequences. Depression, fear reactions, anxiety, traumatic memories, flashbacks, intrusive thoughts, avoidance, grief, sleep disturbances, anger, rumination, episodes of crying, feelings of helplessness and powerlessness, vengeful thinking and planning, disbelief, psychological mutism, precipitation of mania, irritability, dissociation, guilt and feelings of blame, self-loathing and/or self-criticism, suicidal or homicidal thoughts, are a few of the many possible consequences .

These reactions can, of course, occur even without ANY actual physical injury!

The **psychological** consequences of a mishap can potentially affect **many** people, to varying degrees, directly or indirectly, for varying lengths of time, including for a lifetime!

- the driver and/or the driver's family and/or associates
- the passenger and/or his or her family and/or associates

The Driver's Mirror

- the other driver and/or his or her family and/or associates
- the pedestrian victim and/or his or her family and/or associates
- the animal victim's owner and/or family and/or associates
- onlookers or witnesses and/or their families and/or associates
- police personnel and/or their families and/or associates
- rescue personnel and/or their families and/or associates
- medical personnel and/or their families and/or associates
- any sensitive or sympathetic person in receipt of the bad news

The list of persons potentially psychologically affected by a mishap is quite extensive and reflects the nature of human relationships and sensitivity to the circumstances of others. A person's psychological and emotional reactions related to a mishap can have wide reaching and varying effects on those around him or her. Many lives can be ruined from the consequences of one mishap!

The **psychological aftermath** of the following situations can be quite devastating

- in the passenger when the driver dies
- in the passenger when the driver lives, but is medically or psychiatrically disabled
- in the driver when the passenger, other driver, other driver's passenger or pedestrian dies
- in the driver when the passenger, other driver, other driver's passenger or pedestrian is medically or psychiatrically disabled
- in the driver, living with the consequences of a failed suicide attempt
- in the family and/or associates of a successful or unsuccessful vehicular suicide
- in the driver and/or passenger and/or owner when a pet or valued animal is killed

The Driver's Mirror

- in the driver in a driving-under-the-influence situation when the driver or anyone else is killed or injured
- in the driver and/or family and/or associates of an accidental or a deliberate vehicular homicide
- in the driver and/or passenger and/or family and/or associates and/or the property owner when property is damaged in a vehicular mishap
- in the driver and/or passenger and/or family and/or associates when the vehicle is significantly damaged and/or unusable

Illustrative Scenarios

John, age 18, returning from a visit with his ill grandmother, is killed at an uncontrolled intersection by a drunk driver. On hearing the news, his grandmother suffers a fatal heart attack. John's mother, who suffers from depression, relapses with severe depression and suicidal thoughts over the loss of her son and mother, and is hospitalised. John's parents discover that the neighbour's daughter, with whom John was having in a secret relationship, is pregnant.

John's elder brother is so angry at the drunk driver, he threatens to kill him. The family of the drunk driver, ostracised by the community, has to move.

John had been planning to be a doctor.

The drunk driver ends up committing suicide.

The Driver's Mirror

An emergency room doctor tells the following story. "A beautiful young girl was out with her boyfriend, who wanted to show off. He had been drinking and was driving too fast. She asked him repeatedly to slow down but he ignored her. Someone suddenly pulled out of the driveway and he swerved and ran into a tree. He was killed on the spot and she was so badly cut up from broken glass, her face will be scarred for life."

"She was bleeding so profusely we almost lost her. I will never forget it. I have nightmares all the time of not being able to save her."

"I know her doctor, who has told me that she lost most of her friends because of her appearance and has developed panic attacks and depression. She has lost her self-esteem and feels very uncomfortable in public. Her life has been ruined and her family is in constant grief."

A policeman adds, "Accident scenes can be horrendous. Crushed bodies, severed limbs, blood everywhere, screaming and crying victims…. people dying. Most people never actually see such scenes except in educational videos, in movies or in video games. To them, accidents are just an unreal possibility."

"Perhaps repeat speeding offenders should be made to go to accident scenes with emergency personnel, to see these horrible emotionally-traumatic scenes, to shock them into the reality that speed and improper operation of a vehicle are lethal"

"I know lots of officers, ambulance drivers and cleanup personnel, who developed post traumatic stress disorder by having to attend such scenes."

"Even people who drive by and witness the wreckage can be emotionally traumatized. "

The Driver's Mirror

An isolated, lonely, elderly widow only has her husband's dog for company. The dog gets out and is crossing the road when a lone man with an attitude problem spots the dog and deliberately runs over it to kill it. When he sees the dog is not dead, he stops and backs over the animal killing it. This is all witnessed by a neighbor who is horrified and quickly gets the driver's license plate number and calls the police.

By the time the police arrive, the man has long gone.

He is tracked down and charged. His children are beaten up at school by people sympathetic to the old lady.

The widow, extremely upset, stops eating and loses the will to live. The neighbor suffers flashbacks and nightmares and cannot get the scene out of her mind. She becomes a timid driver, because she does not ever want to run over an animal.

Other Aspects of Driving Influenced by Psychology

The Psychology of the Timing and Circumstances of License Acquisition

Although there may be a practical need, because of circumstances, for a person to acquire a driver's license, the decision to postpone the acquisition of the license or to seek acquisition of the license, may be made for various reasons, including psychological reasons.

The Driver's Mirror

A person may **postpone** the acquisition of the license due to

- lack of finances and resources to support the activity
- philosophical, religious or cultural reasons
- awareness of unpreparedness regarding skills, ability and/or knowledge
- lack of confidence or support to take on the challenges of driving
- anxiety problems, disorders and/or fears(rational or irrational) and/or avoidant problems
- having (another) mental illness
- having had a significant other who was killed or disabled in a motor vehicle accident
- having survived a motor vehicle accident as a passenger
- having witnessed a serious motor vehicle accident
- a wish to avoid being stereotyped, based on age
- a significant other's influence regarding driving
- a desire to be independent and not to give in to pressure
- dependency on another person
- availability of a willing assistant/chauffeur and/or public transportation
- insight into having substantial issues which first require resolution

Example.

A young woman really does not want her license, even though her mother is pressuring her to become independent. The girl's father was a very timid man and died in an automobile accident. She has considerable anxiety even thinking about going out into traffic and thinks she needs help before taking the risk. Some of her friends can appreciate her feelings but other peers are making fun of her for being a "chicken". She says she would rather use a bicycle, because it is not polluting, like a 'gas guzzling car'. She thinks she will eventually learn how to drive but wants to make the decision herself.

The Driver's Mirror

A person may eagerly **seek** acquisition of the license due to

- availability of finances and resources to support the activity
- a desire for independence and independent movement
- positive pressure and/or assistance from significant others
- perception of increased maturity, desirability and/or status
- defiance of philosophical, religious or cultural values
- perception of some social or sexual advantage
- unavailability of a willing assistant/chauffeur
- non-availability or limited availability of public transportation
- insightlessness or uncaring regarding issues which might cause another person caution

Example.

A cocky young fellow cannot wait to get his license. In fact he is already driven many times without a license and is looking forward to scoring with the girls, impressing his friends and being able to drive off whenever his parents are fighting. His parents are too busy to care about him and want him out of the house.

Some people who hesitate to get a license would make good drivers, because they are thoughtful, respectful and cautious and some people who rush into getting a license, should not have a license, because they are impulsive, angry, antisocial and/or have serious attitude problems. A prudent person would attend to any problem areas **before** getting a license to drive. Acquiring a driver's license is not a right but a social privilege, with attached responsibilities to operate the vehicle with courtesy, consideration, thoughtfulness, skill and judgment, with awareness of consequences and in accordance with traffic laws and conventions.

The Driver's Mirror

The Psychology of the Timing and Circumstances of Driving Cessation

A prudent, responsible, mature driver would manage personal issues and would drive in such a manner so as not to give anyone cause to question his or her possession of a driver's license.

The psychological impact of having to cease driving may be different depending on whether there is an anticipated **temporary** suspension of the activity or a **permanent** suspension or abandonment of the activity and whether the suspension is voluntary or forced. For example, a medically-ill person who must, for various reasons, cease driving, may be motivated to get well because of the potential to resume this activity in the future. His or her sense of loss/disappointment/anger/frustration may be much less.

The driver is not the only one psychologically and practically affected when driving ceases.

An angry and resentful ex-driver, for example, could project intense feelings into the relationships with significant others, thereby affecting them, or become a complainer about the perceived 'unfairness'/'victimization' or angrily dependent. Practically, someone else may have to assume responsibilities for the transportation needs of the situation or family, for example. Significant others must face the often intense feelings of the former driver or rearrange their lives to accommodate the former driver's restrictions.

Some people are **legally mandated** to stop driving because of their disabilities/illnesses (example, epilepsy), their use of certain sedative medications or because of illegal behaviours and infractions.

The Driver's Mirror

 A certain subset of those people who have had their privileges suspended or canceled will act defiantly and will continue to drive without permission and may continue to endanger themselves and others. Their defiance is itself antisocial and may be based on lack of insight, misdirected anger, an uncaring attitude, personality disorder and/or reliance on excuses. Others will comply, get assistance/therapy/ treatment or will change their attitude/mind-set and will once again be eligible to drive. Some never change and become recidivistic or end up killing someone and/or themselves or are imprisoned.

Despite all the benefits and pleasures of driving, some drivers responsibly and insightfully recognize their impairments, compromises and/or limitations and **voluntarily relinquish** their driver's license. They may be amenable to the observations and requests of others. Such people can admit that, for various reasons, they could inadvertently engage in behaviours dangerous or harmful to themselves or others. They must face the loss of all of the benefits attached to driving and may indeed become despondent or depressed before or after deciding to relinquish their licenses.

The Driver's Mirror

Some have second thoughts and might even drive illegally, without a license, on occasions thereafter. Being caught doing so would be very humiliating for them.

Their loss can be lessened if kind thoughtful persons become available to assist them with their transportation needs or if they have the financial/physical resources to use taxis or public transportation.

Other people are so insightless, defiant or **addicted** to the driving experience, that it may take **serious convincing or coercion to induce them to stop**, when they clearly should, because of their illnesses, disabilities, poor judgment, impairments and/or failing faculties.

Drivers who are dementing are prime examples, as they are often insightless.

Drivers with other conditions such as neurological-illnesses-in-evolution, vertigo and/or dizziness, drug addictions, alcoholism, perceptual problems or attitudinal problems, for example, may insist that they are still safe, capable drivers, even when they are clearly not. On occasion it takes a tragedy for such a driver to finally see that he or she should not be operating a vehicle.

Often loved ones or significant others must resort to strategies such as hiding keys or purposefully disabling the vehicle to prevent the driver from operating the vehicle.

The potential for reusing the vehicle, interpersonal conflict, violence and aggression, arguments, retribution, acting-out or other maladaptive reactions, is substantially likely in this type of situation. The psychological consequence for the driver, the drivers associates or others, can be very significant.

The Driver's Mirror

Example.

A man in his 50s suffers a stroke but recovers, with only mild weakness in his right leg. He insists that he can still drive. While he is driving his wife to the shops, a small child suddenly runs in front of the car and he is just able to stop, because he cannot fully control his right leg. His wife is adamant that he must stop driving, but he says he will just be more cautious.
A few weeks later an aggressive driver, impatient with his caution, tailgates his vehicle, then zooms around with arms waving, threatening him and shouting "Get off the road, ……….!". This upsets him so much, he starts to shake and feels panicky but continues driving.
Again, a small child runs out in front of him but this time he cannot stop and he runs over and kills the child.
His license is permanently taken away by a judge and thereafter, he must live with the shame, guilt and humiliation of having been so proud that it ended in a child's death.
His wife divorces him and she too lives with guilt and depression for not preventing her husband from driving.

The Driver's Mirror

Selection of a Vehicle and Susceptibility to Sales Strategies

A mature, practical driver would decide on the selection of a certain vehicle due to

- the intended use of the vehicle
- known mechanical reliability of the vehicle
- known service costs and ease of serviceability of the vehicle
- known availability of service garages or specialist mechanics
- known reliable source of a used vehicle
- purchase within certain financial parameters

A driver susceptible to the influences of fashion, advertising, astute or clever sales strategies (flattery, acquisition or maintenance of a certain image, status or impression) and/or uncertainty, may choose, or may be influenced to choose, a vehicle based more on his or her psychological issues, preferences, biases, beliefs, philosophies and prejudices, and may end up purchasing a vehicle based on **these** factors more than on **the above practical factors**.

The Driver's Mirror

The Decision to Drive Rather Than Use Public Transportation

People who are forced by circumstances (isolated/remote area, no other driver to rely on) or by the absence of public transportation or by an inadequate public transportation system (inefficient, overcrowded, unsafe, restricted service area/availability), to drive, are, of course, **not** making their choices for psychological reasons.

There also may be practical issues. For example, a mother may need to take her children to the swimming pool at seven o'clock, then to school at half past eight, then go shopping, then go to pay bills or to engage in other activities. For her, using public transportation would be very inefficient.

However, people who, in certain circumstances and for certain activities, have access to inexpensive, reliable, safe, properly-serviced, public transportation or who could walk, ride a bicycle, hire a scooter, rickshaw, motorised tricycle or other conveyance to get to their destination but still insist on driving a vehicle, may be doing so for their own psychological reasons. These could include a desire to maintain a certain image, status or impression, to be separate from the 'masses', to have 'freedom' to come and go at will, to not to have to adhere to a schedule. Some people do not trust others to drive them!

The Driver's Mirror

The following are examples of various situations and problem driving behaviours which could have potentially serious consequences and which may be based on the psychological/personal problems of the offending driver.

Entering a public road

Driver speeds out and continues without concern for an oncoming driver

Driver creeps out slowly when given right of way and thus blocks the courteous driver

Driver blocks the exit or passage of another vehicle in a parking lot or driveway/roadway or of a vehicle emerging from another road/lane/exit

Approaching a traffic-light-regulated intersection

Driver fails to stop or yield

Driver speeds through the intersection without regard for others or against the red light

The Driver's Mirror

Behaviour at a traffic-light-regulated intersection

Driver fails to obey traffic lights

Driver runs a red light

Driver excessively delays continuation on a green light

Driver speeds around a stopped vehicle

Driver behaves aggressively toward a vehicle stopped in front at a red light

Driver races a motorcycle or other vehicle from a stoplight

Driver impatiently turns in front of an oncoming vehicle/motorcycle

Driver blocks the intersection when the traffic light changes, due to impatience in a traffic queue

Driver, in a two-forward-lane situation, changes lanes while turning in an intersection

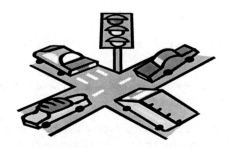

Approaching an unregulated intersection

Driver speeds through the intersection without regard for others

Driver shows excessive caution which blocks others

Driver passes a stopped vehicle

The Driver's Mirror

Behaviour at an unregulated intersection

Driver fails to give way to the right

Driver speeds around a stopped vehicle

Driver speeds through the intersection

Driver behaves aggressively toward a vehicle stopped at the intersection

Negotiating a traffic circle/roundabout

Driver fails/refuses to give way to the prevailing traffic direction

Driver cuts across line markings and thereby forces another vehicle to brake to avoid collision

Driver fails to use signal indicators appropriately

Driver suddenly cuts across lanes to exit instead of going around again to move to outside lane

Driver aggressively intrudes into the roundabout

Driver shows excessive caution or timidity in negotiating the roundabout, which impedes traffic

Driver leaves outside straight-through lane and crosses solid white line to continue around the roundabout, endangering vehicle in inside lane going straight through

The Driver's Mirror

Driving in one-lane-bridge/one-shared-lane situation

Driver ignores a regulatory light controlling access to bridge/lane

Driver aggressively insists on first access to the bridge/lane

Driver forces oncoming vehicle to backup or give way

Driving in a one-way situation

Driver deliberately drives the wrong way down a one-way street

Driver deliberately blocks the entry into or exit from a one-way street

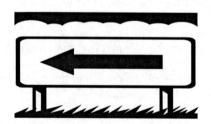

The Driver's Mirror

Driving in a one-forward-lane situation

Driver impatiently tailgates

Driver aggressive passes against an oncoming vehicle

Driver passes on the shoulder of the road

Driver stops suddenly

Driver weaves across the solid center line

Driver passes in a no passing zone

Driver of a slow vehicle (truck, bus, farm vehicle) fails to pull over to let a line of vehicles pass

Driving in a multi-forward-lane situation

Driver zips across lanes without signaling

Driver weaves back and forth between lanes

Driver straddles a lane marker

Driver drives slowly in the inside lane

Driver speeds in the outside lane

Driver passes on the left instead of the right (British System) or on the right instead of the left (Non-British System)

Driver of car/small truck cuts in front of heavy truck/bus/vehicle, endangering self and compromising other driver in emergency stopping situation

Driver or another heavy truck/bus/vehicle drives for some distance beside other such vehicle and thus blocks flow of traffic in inside lane

The Driver's Mirror

Entering an expressway, freeway or dual carriage way

Driver drives slowly on the entrance ramp and fails to achieve the merging speed

Driver speeds around other cars on the entrance ramp

Driver aggressively insinuates into moving traffic

Driver fails to allow incoming vehicle into lane of freeway/motorway

Driver speeds up so another vehicle cannot get in line/or merge with freeway traffic

Driving on an expressway, freeway or dual carriage way

Driver drives more slowly in any lane than conditions permit or than the law allows and thus interferes with the passage of others

Driver drives slowly in the inside lane and fails to move over to the outside lane and thus interferes with the passage of others

Driver drives in the inside lane, side by side with another vehicle, to block progress of other vehicles in the inside lane

Driver of truck or vehicle with a boat/trailer/caravan drives slowly in the inside lane and will not move into the outside lane

Approaching a merging-lane situation

Driver speeds up to the very end of a merging lane to get ahead of others

Driver causes a problem merging into a slower/faster situation by
    Unnecessary stopping
    Aggressive forcing into traffic flow

The Driver's Mirror

Exiting an expressway, freeway or dual carriage way

Driver fails to plan ahead to exit the freeway

Driver intrudes into the outside lane "at the last second" to enter the off ramp

Driver in the outside lane will not let a signaling driver into the outside lane to exit the freeway

Driver aggressively speeds past vehicles on the off ramp

Driver just off freeway, continues to speed in a lower speed zone

Bus/train/airport drop-off/pickup situations

Driver stops in a designated taxi/ bus or van stop, thus blocking the designated vehicle

Driver blocks access to the designated drop-off/pickup location

Driver blocks exit from the designated drop-off/pickup location

Driver speeds through the area designated for drop-off /pickup

Driver ignores right of way at designated pedestrian crosswalk

Driver is slow to enter or exit designated drop-off/pickup location and thereby impedes others

Driver straddles lanes thus impeding another driver

Driver stops in a non-designated drop-off/pickup location and thus impedes other drivers

The Driver's Mirror

Designated parking parallel to a one- or two-forward-lane situation

Inexperienced driver takes excessive time and/or attempts to successfully park

Next-in-line driver prevents driver from reverse parking by blocking the parking spot

Next-in-line driver drives into the parking spot, taking it from the reverse-parking driver

Oncoming driver crosses into the parking spot on opposite side of road in a dangerous maneuver

Driver parks so as to deny another driver a parking spot, by straddling a designated space

Driver impatiently speeds around a vehicle attempting to park, endangering an oncoming vehicle

Driver parks in such a way as to prevent another vehicle from leaving its parking bay

The Driver's Mirror

Undesignated parking parallel to a one- or two-forward-lane situation

Driver parks in an illegal zone

Driver parks in a dangerous location and partially or totally blocks a lane

Driver parks so as to deny another driver a parking spot

Driver impatiently speeds around a vehicle attempting to park, endangering an oncoming vehicle

Parking in a designated parking lot/garage with designated bays

Driver parks so as to deny another driver a parking spot by straddling a designated space

Driver aggressively takes a parking spot for which another driver has been waiting

Driver parks excessively close to another vehicle preventing door-opening and entrance into or exit from the vehicle

Parking in a designated parking lot/garage with undesignated bays

Driver parks at an unusual angle or position to deny space for another vehicle/other vehicles

Driver aggressively takes a parking spot for which another driver has been waiting

Driver parks excessively close to another vehicle preventing door-opening and entrance into or exit from the vehicle

The Driver's Mirror

Parking in a reverse-in-angle-parking situation

Inexperienced driver takes excessive time and/or attempts to successfully park

Next-in-line driver prevents driver from reverse-parking by blocking the parking spot

Driver parks so as to deny another driver a parking spot by straddling a designated space

Driver impatiently speeds around a vehicle attempting to park, endangering an oncoming vehicle

Driver parks excessively close to another vehicle preventing door-opening and entrance into or exit from the vehicle

Parking in an undesignated-parking situation

Driver parks without permission on someone's lawn or personal property

Driver parks and blocks a driveway or exit/entrance

Driver parks in a dangerous location and partially or totally blocks a lane

Driver parks in pedestrian-crosswalk/ school-crosswalk location

Driver parks on a highway median

Driver parks on the freeway off-ramp/on-ramp

Driver parks in a limited-visibility location on a winding mountainous road

The Driver's Mirror

Parking on a hill/ steep slope

Driver fails to apply parking brake or put vehicle in appropriate gear on the slope

Driver fails to angle the tires into the curb and the vehicle rolls forward or backward causing damage and endangerment

Driver parks too close to another vehicle

Other parking situations

Driver, without authorised license plate or appropriate sticker, parks in a disabled-parking bay

Driver parks in an exclusion zone around a fire hydrant

Driver parks in a clearway outside of parking hours

Other circumstances

Driver uses the horn excessively and unnecessarily

Driver does not use seatbelt or proper safety seats/restraints for self/passengers/children/animals

Driver operates the vehicle with children or animal on his or her lap

Driver fails to get right off roadway when stopping

Driver does a wide turn into another lane/driveway

Driver tail-gaits at any speed

The Driver's Mirror

Driver leaves huge gap in front, in slow traffic

Driver speeds on the shoulder past a line of traffic

Driver drives at excessive speeds in rain, snow, sleet or fog

Driver fails to use signal indicators

Driver misuses signal indicators

Driver slows down unnecessarily when something is happening at the roadside

Driver keeps letting other vehicles in front in a line

Driver or passenger throws objects out of a moving vehicle, endangering others

Driver drives machinery, farm implements, carts, livestock in a manner which impedes traffic

Driver of heavy truck/bus/large vehicle tailgates and/or drives aggressively toward other vehicles

Driver of non-police, non-emergency vehicle with emergency light systems drives as if all others should give way

Driver proceeds on in situations with limited visibility, such as in heavy rain, fog, snow storm, thus endangering the vehicle, others and property

Driver fails to give way to pedestrians or animals on road

The Driver's Mirror

Off-road driver takes unnecessary risks on slopes and/or unstable surfaces and rolls or mires vehicle

Driver veers onto a soft surface and bogs the vehicle, due to misuse of the accelerator

Driver takes unnecessary risks driving on ice and the vehicle falls through the ice or spins out of control

Driver fails to determine the depth of the water and proceeds and the vehicle becomes stuck or flooded

Driver fails to take precautions and drives into flowing water and the vehicle is swept away

Driver attempts to negotiate an abandoned bridge and the vehicle falls through

Driver attempts to or drives on a railroad track

Driver deliberately attempts to negotiate stairs, narrow ramp, tunnel or alley

Driver speeds over a railroad crossing to beat the boom and/or train

Driver drives despite being ill prepared, impaired, ill, intoxicated, full of emotion, (see above)

The Driver's Mirror

Driver drives at excessive speeds on an unsealed road surface, such as on gravel

Driver passes/overtakes in an unsafe location and/or with insufficient passing space

Driver passes/overtakes another vehicle over a continuous unbroken white line

Driver passes an oversized vehicle and inserts between that vehicle and the pilot vehicle

Female driver alone or with young children, shows poor judgment in picking up male hitchhiker not known to her

Lone male driver shows poor judgment in picking up female hitchhiker, who could falsely allege sexual assault

Driver makes a U-turn on a multi-lane freeway over the median or performs another illegal U-turn

Driver drives in an unlimited-speed situation (for example, German autobahn)

- in a vehicle in less-than-optimal mechanical condition
- beyond his/her skill or experience level

Driver fails to obey arrows or markings on the roadway

Driver drives in a bus or special-purpose lane

Driver drives some distance in another driver's blind spot

The Driver's Mirror

Antisocial driving behaviours

Driver engages in **any** dangerous, illegal and/or discourteous driving behaviours with children and/or young adolescents in the vehicle who could learn similar behaviour through role modeling or be harmed

Driver knowingly drives in the compromised mental/emotional and/or physical state

Driver operates the vehicle without a license

Driver drives outside the terms and conditions of a learner's or provisional license

Driver drives with a suspended license

Driver knowingly drinks excessive alcohol and drives

Driver deliberately uses mind-altering drugs and drives

Driver tail-gaits at high speed

Driver drives with falsified identification/license plate/certificate of registration

Driver uses another person's identification

Driver provides a false name or another person's name to a police officer

Driver deliberately slows in an attempt to force the following driver to stop

The Driver's Mirror

Driver stops and blocks the road, forcing an oncoming vehicle to stop

Driver giving nasty looks and stares to other drivers to intimidate them

Driver weaves in and out of traffic at high speed, with or without the use of signal lights

Driver rapidly approaches vehicle ahead using aggressive maneuvers to coerce other driver out of the way

- flashing lights
- blowing horn
- gesturing

Driver engages in high speed driving with police or other vehicle in pursuit or to pursue another vehicle

Driver tries to force or forces another vehicle off the road

Driver cuts in front of another vehicle

Driver deliberately nudges another vehicle

Driver runs into and physically moves another vehicle to pass, thereby damaging it

Driver uses the vehicle to deliberately try to harm/kill someone

Driver scratches another person's vehicle deliberately to cause damage

Driver breaks another owner's vehicle window, mirror, headlight, or tail light

Driver removes parts from another person's vehicle

Driver steals another person's vehicle

Driver drives without headlights activated at appropriate/mandated times

The Driver's Mirror

Driver knowingly drives a malfunctioning vehicle

- poor brakes
- accelerator sticks or malfunctions
- cracked or broken windscreen and/or side mirrors
- no signal lights
- malfunctioning signal lights
- malfunctioning headlamps

Driver pulls/swerves out in front of oncoming motorcycle or vehicle, forcing the other driver to slow or stop

Driver tries to frighten or run into pedestrians

Driver deliberately runs down or runs over animals on road

Driver drives

- over fragile natural environmental features without a care for the damage created
- over another person's property causing deliberate damage or destruction
- down a sidewalk, public path or into a pedestrian mall
- over parkland, golf course, protected area, nature preserve and/or beach without permission

Driver drives dangerously at, near or through a public event, such as a parade, march, bicycle or foot race

Driver ignores speed limit in school zones

Driver flashes lights at oncoming vehicle to warn of speed trap and thereby condones/facilitates speeding by other drivers

Driver fails to obey crossing guard at school crossing

Driver deliberately parks in a delivery zone

The Driver's Mirror

Driver negotiates a designated pedestrian crosswalk in a dangerous manner

Driver avoids paying road tolls and/or fines and/or speeding/parking tickets

Driver interacts with a pedestrian in a dangerous manner

Driver interacts with a bicyclist/motorcyclist in a dangerous manner

Driver fails to give emergency, police and official vehicles the right-of-way

Driver blocks access to a boat ramp on purpose

Driver deliberately leaves vehicle and trailer on a boat ramp, thus blocking it

Driver uses vehicle in an illegal activity, such as drive-by shooting, robbery or hijacking/kidnapping

Driver is involved in or causes a crash/pedestrian mishap and fails to stop or stay at the scene

Driver fails to report a crash or serious incident

Driver fails to dim high-beam lights when approaching or closely following a vehicle

Driver engages in deliberate disruptive or frightening behaviours to scare horses, oxen or other beasts of burden, or allows passenger(s) to do so, putting riders, handlers, cargo and/or property at risk

Driver or passenger tosses bottles or trash out of the vehicle into the public domain

Driver or passenger deliberately throws lit cigarette or other incendiary object or other object or substance into another vehicle

The Driver's Mirror

Non-courteous driving behaviours

Driver rudely gesturing at other drivers

Driver feigning ignorance or stupidity to induce other drivers to allow an indulgence

Driver expects another driver to let his/her vehicle in line but does not acknowledge the courtesy

Driver does not acknowledge a courtesy extended to him/her by another driver

Driver drives to prevent motorcycle/vehicle from passing

Interactions with Police

Driver fails to obey police instructions

Driver argues with/verbally abuses a police officer

Driver attempts to assault/kill a police officer

Driver attempts to run over a police officer

Driver deliberately rams/damages a police car

Driver attempts to evade/escape from police

Driver gives false information to a police officer

Driver impersonates a police officer

The Driver's Mirror

Driver is sexually abusive to a police officer

Driver attempts to use gender, notoriety, bribery and/or threats to manipulate a police officer

Interactions with emergency/military personnel/vehicles and/or road workers

Driver fails to give way to and/or obstructs emergency/military vehicles

Driver fails to obey lawful directions of emergency/military personnel and/or road workers

The Driver's Mirror

Driver drives so as to endanger emergency/military and/or road workers

Driver unlawfully speeds to keep up to emergency vehicles

Emergency situations – (not everyone in the world has a mobile phone!)

Driver fails to ask if another driver requires assistance in an emergency situation

Driver fails to render assistance to another driver in an emergency situation

Driver acts-out toward/endangers the driver of a vehicle which has broken down on the road

Driver preys upon the driver of a broken down vehicle

Driver feigns a breakdown to prey upon a would-be Good Samaritan/helper

Driver decides not to assist another driver who has had an accident after that driver just having acted-out in some manner

The Driver's Mirror

Natural emergency situations

- Hurricane/Typhoon
- Tornado/Waterspout
- Ice storm
- Snow blizzard
- Heavy rain
- Hail storm
- Fire
- Flood
- Mud slide
- Rockwall collapse/falling rocks
- Tsunami
- Avalanche

Driver decides to take risks in dangerous and potentially life-threatening situations

Driver endangers others through his or her own risk-taking decisions

Driver shows poor judgment in not appreciating serious risks and endangers self and others

The Driver's Mirror

Driver fails to find shelter for self and vehicle

Driver fails to get far off the road to wait out the storm

Driver has not prepared the vehicle nor items in the vehicle for emergencies

Driver continues to use high-beam lights in fog, heavy snow or smoke

Problem Driving Behaviours Which Reveal Biases and Prejudices

Due to the complex nature and meaning of the driving experience, the driver may reveal in that activity, the true biases or prejudices which he or she may hold and not reveal or admit to at other times. No matter what a person may **say** to others, the internal dialogue and private thoughts of the person/driver in reaction to the other driver, the vehicle type, the vehicle characteristics/adornment, the cargo, the occupant(s), reveal the **TRUE** prejudices of the person/driver.

The following are some examples, which, like all the other examples, are meant to provoke increased awareness, insight and self-reflection, regarding driving behaviour and mentality.

The Driver's Mirror

Sexist driving

Male driver is aggressive, pushy and/or shows off

Female driver is aggressive, pushy and/or shows off

Female/male driver speeds under assumption she/he can use charms/gender to escape consequences of her/his behavior when dealing with a police officer of the opposite gender

Female/male driver does not let other driver in line due to other driver's gender

Female/male driver lets other driver in line due to other driver's gender

Female/male driver acts-out toward another driver because of his/her gender

Female/male driver only shows courtesy toward driver of same/other gender

Female/male driver only shows discourtesy/aggression toward driver of same/other gender

The Driver's Mirror

Racist/culturally-biased driving

Driver has an adverse reaction to another driver when he/she perceives this person to be of a different race or cultural group and acts-out

Driver from a minority group acts-out issues while operating a vehicle

Driver from a majority group acts-out toward a driver from a minority group or vice versa

Driver uses unresolved racial/group issues to justify acting-out while operating a vehicle or toward other drivers

Age issues

Driver reacts to/acts-out toward another driver, based on that other driver's perceived age

Driver drives in such a way as to frighten or compromise very young or very old passenger

Driver drives in such a way as to endanger self and others

The Driver's Mirror

Other Cues to Which the Driver May React with Bias, Prejudice, Acting-Out or Problem Behaviours

Religious

Driver's reactions and problem behaviours are evoked by seeing the other driver's dress and/or religious items/symbols displayed in or on the vehicle.

Educational

Driver's reactions and problem behaviours are evoked by seeing the other driver's personal characteristics/dress and/or items displayed in or on the vehicle, such as school/University stickers, emblems, banners or symbols.

Wealth

Driver's reactions and problem behaviours are evoked by seeing the other driver's dress and/or vehicle make model or condition

Occupation

Driver's reactions and problem behaviours are evoked by seeing the other driver's dress, vehicle type, business emblems, cargo and/or occupational items displayed in or on the vehicle

The Driver's Mirror

Activity

Driver's reactions and problem behaviours are evoked by seeing the dress or behaviour of the other vehicle's driver or passenger(s) (such as pointing fingers or cameras) or seeing specific items being transported (such as leisure or other equipment, guns, boats or machinery) which might indicate the pursuit of a certain activity.

License Status

Driver's reactions and problem behaviours are evoked by seeing the other driver's 'Learner' or 'Probationary' status.

The 'Learner' or 'Probationary' driver's interest in and focus on **other** 'Learner' or 'Probationary' drivers, may distract the 'Learner' or 'Probationary' driver and lead to accidents or problem situations.

This general principle can also apply in the other examples above or in other situations.

Alternatively, instead of showing tolerance, accommodation, kindness or understanding of the anxieties and cautiousness of a new driver, a problem driver could attempt to deliberately frighten, intimidate or punish the less experienced driver and/or show no patience or thoughtfulness, as the inexperienced driver executes some maneuver, such as parking, merging or entering a freeway, for example.

The Driver's Mirror

When the 'Learner' or 'Probationary' driver is the victim of a problem driver's inconsiderate, rude, aggressive or dangerous behaviours, various consequences could result.

- The 'Learner' or 'Probationary' driver may become even more timid, cautious, anxious or frightened and this could have a negative effect on his or her behaviour and on the safety of his or her driving.

- The 'Learner' or 'Probationary' driver may decide, once more confident and experienced, to 'get back' at other drivers for their lack of consideration, and thus perpetuate problem driving and interactions.

This general principle can also apply in the other examples above or in other situations.

The Driver's Mirror

Driving-Contemplation Checklist

Weather

- Is the nature or severity of the weather such that driving would be too risky or unsafe?

No - Consider the other issues

Yes - DO NOT DRIVE, make other plans

Familiarity with the vehicle

- **Am I familiar and practiced enough with the vehicle to operate it safely ?**

No - Take time to become familiarized with the vehicle or to get assistance/practice before operating the vehicle in a public area.

Yes - Consider the other issues

The Driver's Mirror

Roadworthiness of the vehicle

- Is there anything about the current status of the vehicle likely to compromise its safe operation? (Lights, tyres, windscreen, engine, mirrors, contents of vehicle)

No - Consider the other issues

Yes - Consider repairing the compromised component(s) and/or removal of visual obstructions, prior to operation of vehicle

Clothing and footwear

- Is there anything about my clothing or footwear which could compromise the safe operation of the vehicle? (Clothing too tight/ loose, footwear too tight/loose, inappropriate footwear, broken/ dirty glasses, glasses wrong prescription, no sunglasses, sunglasses too dark)

No - Consider the other issues

Yes - Correct the problem before operating the vehicle

The Driver's Mirror

Physical status

- Is there any pain, physical discomfort, perceptual problem, neurological problem, back discomfort, or other medical issue which could compromise the safe operation of vehicle ?

No - Consider the other issues

Yes - Correct, if possible, prior to driving but if cannot be corrected, DO NOT DRIVE and make alternative arrangements!

Mental status

- Is there anything about my mental status which could compromise my ability to drive safely, compromise my attitude, lessen my capacity for courtesy, influence my adherence to road rules or influence the way I interact with other drivers? (Tiredness, drowsiness, disorientation, poor concentration, forgetfulness, anger, rage, irritability, anxiety, distractibility, depression, suicidal or homicidal thoughts, hearing voices, seeing things, paranoid thoughts, feeling controlled/compelled, fearfulness, crying, dissociation, sadness, derealisation, flashbacks, intense grief,

The Driver's Mirror

feelings of unconcern/ hopelessness/ futility, defiant/vengeful/critical/derisive/ predatory thoughts, impatience, thoughts of superiority/inferiority, feeling stressed/ pressured, or thinking I am being used/ manipulated/taken-for-granted/punished/ inconvenienced, or other negative thoughts or perceptions)

No – **Am I sure?** I must be honest and read the above list again!

Dishonesty now will only compromise my life or the life of someone else!

(If you <u>are</u> sure, you may be one of the <u>few people</u> on the road who should be there!)

Yes - If I think the compromise is temporary, can I postpone driving until I am calm, focused, alert and have the right mental attitude? If not,

DO NOT DRIVE.
Please make other arrangements.

The Driver's Mirror

Yes- If I think the compromise has been present for some time, or may continue, why am I even thinking of driving and what am I going to do about the issue(s)?! I may need sleep, evaluation by a doctor, compliance with my medication, psychotherapy, or a good talking to by a Judge, to remind me of my obligations as a citizen !

Other vehicle occupants

- Am I transporting animals?

No - Consider the other issues

Yes - Make sure each animal is properly caged or tethered/restrained for safety before driving

The Driver's Mirror

- **Am I transporting children?**

No - Consider the other issues

Yes - Small babies and children <u>must</u> be transported in approved safety seats. If these are not available, the baby/child/small children should not ride. Older children should use approved seatbelts and remain seated at all times.

- **Am I transporting a smoker?**

No - Consider the other issues

Yes - A smoker should be asked to refrain from smoking in the vehicle, especially if pets/animals or children are being transported. Not only does smoke damage their sensitive lungs, a smoker could accidentally set fire to clothing or other material in the vehicle.

If a smoker refuses to refrain from smoking, he or she should be invited to use alternative transportation.

The Driver's Mirror

- Am I transporting a medically or psychiatrically ill person?

    No - Consider the other issues

    Yes - If the person is likely to require my attention, cause a disturbance or attempt to exit the moving vehicle en route, I need to consider a chaperone, police or ambulance assistance, for everyone's safety.

    If I am personally quite upset or agitated about the situation, perhaps I should get someone to drive me to the destination!

Thank you very much for being a responsible driver!

The Driver's Mirror

CONCLUSION

When things go right, driving can be a very pleasurable experience. It is however also a very serious activity in which maturity, responsibility, thoughtfulness, preparation, good judgment, well-managed emotions and impulses, consideration for others, a law-abiding attitude, minimisation of compromises and the capacity to make rapid decisions and to be aware of consequences, are essential. Even the slightest misjudgment can result in a catastrophe with far-reaching financial, practical, social, physical and/or emotional consequences.

Although the list of problem situations or issues is not exhaustive, it is meant to be a thought-provoking reminder of responsibilities and consequences and of the compromising, unacceptable, inappropriate, dangerous, illegal, ill-considered or badly-managed instances where emotional, physical and/or personal harm to self or others or destruction of property could occur.

Knowing more about your own psychology and that of others, being aware of your limitations and the limitations of your vehicle, exercising good judgment at all times, being courteous and thoughtful behind the wheel and respecting the rights of others to share the pleasures and privilege of driving, will make the driving experience a safe and less stressful one.

It would be mature and responsible for a prospective or already-licensed driver to admit to having personal problems, problem attitudes, conflicts with others, unresolved prejudices or other psychological issues, limitations or burdens, physical or mental illness and to seek out psychotherapy, counseling or treatment, so these issues are **not** brought into the driving experience.

Problem recidivistic drivers should accept the need for involvement in special driving-offender programs to rehabilitate their approach to the whole driving experience.

The Driver's Mirror

Please help make driving a safe, pleasant and rewarding social and personal experience!

Please consult any of a huge variety of Psychology and Self Help Books currently available, to gain further knowledge, understanding, and mastery of issues raised in this manual.

Use of a dictionary, encyclopedia or the Internet will help with the understanding of technical words.

Thank You !!

Dr. Elwin G. Upton, M.D., F.R.C.P.(C.)

Illustrations from Public Domain Clip Art and Microsoft Clip Art with thanks to those sources and artists.

Lightning Source UK Ltd.
Milton Keynes UK
UKOW041117210612

194818UK00006B/12/P